Śrī Dakṣiṇāmūrti Stotram

of Śrī Śaṅkarācārya

Dedicated to My Teacher

Parama Pujya Sri Sri Sri
Swami Dayananda Saraswati

Rediscovering Indian Literary Classics, no. 10

Śrī Dakṣiṇāmūrti Stotram
of Śrī Śaṅkarācārya

With the commentary
Tattva Prakāśikā

by
Swami Tattvavidananda Saraswati

Edited by
Puppala B.

D.K. Printworld (P) Ltd.
New Delhi

Cataloging in Publication Data — DK

Tattvavidananda Saraswati, *Swami*, 1948 –
Śri Dakṣiṇāmūrti stotram of Śrī Śaṅkarācārya.
(Rediscovering Indian literary classics, no. 10)

1. Śaṅkarācārya. Dakṣiṇāmūrtistotram. 2. Siva (Hindu deity) — Prayer-books and devotions — Sanskrit. 3. Advaita. 4. Hindu hymns, Sanskrit — History and criticism. I. Śaṅkarācārya. Dakṣiṇāmūrtistotram. English & Sanskrit. II. Puppala, B. III. Title. IV. Series: Rediscovering Indian literary classics; no. 10.

ISBN 81-246-0210-7 (Hardbound)
ISBN 81-246-0235-2 (Paperback)

First Published in India in 2002
Second impression, 2003
Third impression, 2007

Printed and published by:
D.K. Printworld (P) Ltd.
Regd. office : *'Sri Kunj'*, F-52, Bali Nagar
Ramesh Nagar Metro Station
New Delhi - 110 015
Phones : (011) 2545-3975, 2546-6019
Fax : (011) 2546-5926
E-mail : dkprintworld@vsnl.net
Web : www.dkprintworld.com

Editor's Note

The present work, *Dakṣiṇāmūrti Stotram*, is based on the talks given by Swami Tattvavidananda Saraswati to the students of Arsha Vidya Sagar during the year 2000. The talks have been recorded and transcribed in hand and later typed on the computer and the basic text was prepared. The text has been thoroughly revised by Swamiji incorporating Sanskrit verses along with the translation, transliteration and their word to word meanings.

It has been a unique experience in transcribing, reading, and reviewing the text. For those of us who received the teaching sitting at the feet of Swamiji, it has been a transformation, which no words can adequately describe. We had felt that Dakṣiṇāmūrti Himself has come down in form of Swamiji to teach us the sacred texts. We also experience total cessation of *saṁsāra* during the *śravaṇa* of Swamiji's exposition of the Śāstra and a gradual dilution of that *saṁsāra* in our life.

This book is unique from several standpoints:

1. The text has been presented in a manner to expound the ultimate Truth and take the reader to that Truth through a variety of experiences of the false individual in the web of *saṁsāra* woven around oneself and then negating the false person and sublating him in that *Akhaṇḍa Caitanya*.

2. The experiences related are so common and striking that one can discriminate the real from the unreal and discover the substratum, the ultimate reality of all Existence.

3. Arriving at the Truth through several original, imaginative, and contemporary examples. One such imaginative example (taken by Swamiji from his own teacher, Sri Swami Dayananda Saraswatiji) is a ball of wool out of which an embroidery is fashioned depicting human beings, animals, birds, rivers, mountains, sky, etc., and the same embroidery turns into the thread when the hang of the thread is pulled comparing the wool to the undifferentiated *Māyā* with Awareness as substratum and manifesting the whole universe of living and non-living beings.

4. Guidance to the *sādhaka* through various stages of *sādhanā* in addition to bringing out the purport of the *Stotram*. One such *sādhanā* is to develop an attitude of witness, *sākṣitva*, to the inner world of feelings, emotions, insult, esteem, etc., and constant appreciation of the outer world as a manifestation of the Ultimate Reality (*Viśvarūpa Upāsanā*).

Some other highlights of the text are:

1. Elaborate introduction tracing the sources of the *Dakṣiṇāmūrti Stotram* to the *Sūta Saṁhitā* of the *Skanda Purāṇa* and Śaṅkara's deep study of the same; and writing the *Stotram*, after completing *Brahmasūtra Bhāṣya*, makes it an unsurpassed Vedānta text of brevity.

2. The significance and uniqueness of *mauna vyākhyā* of Dakṣiṇāmūrti.

3. Theories of creation, both ancient as well as the modern, such as Big Bang theory, Steady State theory and their basic inadequacy in explaining the nature of the universe as against the conclusion of Vedānta that the creation is a manifestation of the unmanifest in the framework of time-space-causation.

4. Discussion on the contentions of various schools of philosophy regarding the nature of *Ātman*.

5. The unreality and the divisive perspective of the relationships such as between the cause and the effect, the master and the servant, the student and the teacher, the father and the son, etc., leading to the bondage of *saṁsāra*.

6. *Aṣṭamūrti Upāsanā* leading to *sarvātma bhāva* and what *upāsanā* means at the level of the sense-organs, organs of action, mind, intellect, and ego.

7. How *śravaṇa*, *manana*, *nididhyāsana*, etc., can lead one to gain the over-lordship and its fruits in addition to Self-Knowledge.

8. The continuity obtaining through the various stages of life such as childhood, old age, etc., and the waking, dream, and deep sleep states is none other than the *Caitanya* in which they appear.

Sri Swamiji says that he is indebted to many Mahātmās like Sri Nisargadatta Maharaj, in addition to his own teacher, whose teachings inspired him, not only in his personal pursuit but also in his teaching of Vedānta to seekers.

I thank Sri Mohan Bhujale, Holmdel, New Jersey (a student of Swamiji in US) for very helpful suggestions in the body of the text. I also thank my son Jagannathrao, and Shri V. Venkatrao, a longtime student of Swamiji, for the devoted and hard work in typing the whole text on the computer.

Suggestions for improvements in the text in any manner are most welcome.

August 22, 2001 **B Puppala**
Ganesh Chaturthi
Secunderabad

Contents

Key to Transliteration

Key to Transliteration and Pronunciation of Sanskrit Letters

Since Sanskrit is a highly phonetic language, accuracy in articulation of the letters is important. For those unfamiliar with the Devanāgarī script, the international transliteration is a guide to the proper pronunciation of Sanskrit letters.

अ *a* (but)	ङ *ṅa* (sing)[1]	न *na* (numb)[4]
आ *ā* (mom)	च *ca* (chunk)[2]	प *pa* (spin)[5]
इ *i* (it)	छ* *cha* (catch him)[2]	फ* *pha* (loophole)[5]
ई *ī* (beet)	ज *ja* (john)[2]	ब *ba* (bin)[5]
उ *u* (put)	झ *jha* (hedgehog)[2]	भ *bha* (abhor)[5]
ऊ *ū* (pool)	ञ *ña* (bunch)[2]	म *ma* (much)[5]
ऋ *ṛ* (rhythm)	ट *ṭa* (start)[3]	य *ya* (young)
ए *e* (play)	ठ* *ṭha* (anthill)[3]	र *ra* (drama)
ऐ *ai* (high)	ड *ḍa* (dart)[3]	ल *la* (luck)
ओ *o* (toe)	ढ* *ḍha* (godhead)[3]	व *va* (vile)
औ *au* (loud)	ण *ṇa* (under)[3]	श *śa* (shove)
क *ka* (skate)[1]	त *ta* (path)[4]	ष *ṣa* (bushel)
ख* *kha* (blokhead)[1]	थ *tha* (thunder)[4]	स *sa* (so)
ग *ga* (gate)[1]	द *da* (that)[4]	ह *ha* (hum)
घ *gha* (loghut)[1]	ध* *dha* (breathe)[4]	

ं *ṁ* *anusvāra* (nasalisation of preceding vowel)

: *ḥ* *visarga* (aspiration of preceding vowel)

* No exact English equivalents for these letters.

[1] guttural

[2] palatal

[3] lingual

[4] dental

[5] labial

Śrī Gaṇeśāya Namaḥ

Śrī Dakṣiṇāmūrti Stotram with the commentary *Tattva Prakāśikā*

Introduction

DAKṢIṆĀMŪRTI is an incarnation of Lord Śiva. The Lord has many names like Śiva, Viṣṇu, etc. The Lord is called Śiva because he is *maṅgala svarūpa*, that is, all-auspiciousness. The Lord is also called Viṣṇu, because of being *sarva-vyāpaka*, all-pervading. The entire universe has got its existence in *Īśvara*. Hence *Īśvara* is called Viṣṇu. Dakṣiṇāmūrti is an incarnation of the Lord. Every incarnation has a special purpose. *Jīva*, the individual, takes birth by virtue of *karma*s performed in earlier lives. Those *karma*s of the *jīva* that have matured bring forth a life form for the *jīva*; that of a human being or any other life form. In the case of *Īśvara*, the situation is entirely different. *Īśvara* takes up a life form by his own will (*svecchā*), for accomplishing a special purpose. This purpose is two-fold as described by Bhagavān himself in the *Gītā* (4-8):

> परित्राणाय साधूनां विनाशाय च दुष्कृताम् ।
> धर्मसंस्थापनार्थाय संभवामि युगे युगे ।। (४-८)
>
> *paritrāṇāya sādhūnāṁ vināśāya ca duṣkṛtām* ।
> *dharmasaṁsthāpanārthāya sambhavāmi yuge yuge* ।।
>
> For the protection of those who are committed to *dharma*, for the destruction (conversion) of those who follow *adharma*, and for the establishment of *dharma*, I come into being in every age.

This *dharma* is two-fold: *karma* (action) and *jñāna* (knowledge). It is said:

वेदोऽखिलो धर्ममूलम् ।

vedo'khilo dharmamūlam ।

The entire Veda is the source of *dharma* (righteous conduct).

Śrī Śaṅkara says in his introduction to *Gītā*:

स द्विविधो हि वेदोक्तो धर्मः प्रवृत्तिलक्षणो निवृत्तिलक्षणश्च ।

sa dvividho hi vedokto dharmaḥ pravṛttilakṣaṇo nivṛttilakṣaṇaśca ।

That *dharma* is two-fold: righteous activity and withdrawal from it by knowledge.

The body of knowledge called the Veda is the repository of *dharma*. The Veda is broadly divided into two sections. The first section is *karma-kāṇḍa*, which teaches activity-based *dharma*. It is also called *pravṛtti dharma*. The second portion of the Veda teaches a totally different kind of *dharma*, called *ātma-dharma*. It is also called *nivṛtti dharma* (withdrawal from activity by the knowledge that *ātman* is not the agent of actions). Strategic advance into the world is *dharma*; so also deliberate withdrawal from the world is *dharma*. On the eleventh day of the lunar cycle, namely, on *Ekādaśī* day, fasting is *dharma*, while on the next day, that is *Dvādaśī*, taking food early in the morning is *dharma*.

Dharma is normally taken care of by the society. However, when *dharma* declines in the society and *adharma* increases, corrective measures have to be taken. In such a situation Bhagavān comes forth and corrects the imbalance. Correction of the imbalance is also two-fold. In case of *pravṛtti dharma*, Bhagavān comes in the form of *avatāra*, an incarnation and He punishes the wicked and rewards the virtuous. That is what, for example, Lord Rāma has done and we have quite a few such *avatāra*-s like *Matsya*, *Kūrma*, etc.

Ātma-dharma also declines over a period of time. Lord Śrī Kr̥ṣṇa explained this in the *Gītā* in the following verse:

एवं परंपराप्राप्तमिमं राजर्षयो विदुः ।
स कालेनेह महता योगो नष्टः परंतप ।।
— *श्रीमद्भगवद्गीता*, ४-२

evaṁ paramparāprāptamimaṁ rājarṣayo viduḥ ।
sa kāleneha mahatā yogo naṣṭaḥ parantapa ।।
— *Śrīmadbhagavad-Gītā*, 4-2

This lineage of two-fold *dharma* started with the originator of the universe, namely *hiraṇyagarbha*, and percolated down into the human society through the great kings who were seers and sages in their own right. However, this *dharma* declined over a long period of time.

Dharma can never be destroyed. It only disappears temporarily. Some people claim that Sanskrit is a dead language. This is not correct. The fact is that the language is not in common use. But even that situation is quickly changing and once again Sanskrit is becoming popular. In the same way, this *ātma-dharma* also declines in certain times. On such occasions, Bhagavān appears in a suitable incarnation and makes it prominent through his teachings. The Lord appeared in the incarnation of Śrī Kr̥ṣṇa and took care of *pravr̥tti dharma* by killing the wicked persons like Kaṁsa. He further re-established *dharma* by way of teaching the *Gītā* to Arjuna. This is why Śrī Kr̥ṣṇa is called *jagad-guru*, the teacher for the entire humanity. There is an interesting difference between the incarnations of Śrī Rāma and Śrī Kr̥ṣṇa. The sage Vasiṣṭha teaches to Rāma: *Tat-tvam-asi*, that (the supreme reality) art thou. But Śrī Kr̥ṣṇa often proclaims himself thus: *aham brahmāsmi*, I am the Supreme reality of this universe.

Certain *avatāra*s like Śrī Rāma are meant to protect the *pravṛtti dharma* exclusively. Certain others like Śrī Kṛṣṇa *avatāra* protected both *pravṛtti* as well as *nivṛtti dharma*. In the present context, the incarnation of the Lord as Dakṣiṇāmūrti is meant for safeguarding *ātma-dharma* exclusively. This *avatāra* of the Lord is described in the *Sūta Saṁhitā* of the *Skanda Purāṇa*. The *Skanda Purāṇa* is a voluminous treatise, almost as big as the *Mahābhārata* (one hundred thousand verses). The *Sūta Saṁhitā* constitutes a moderately big section of that Purāṇa. The sage Sūta is said to have taught many a Purāṇa in the *satrayāga*s (elaborate community rituals) performed by the sages of *naimiṣa* forest during the intervals between various parts of the lengthy ritual. The *Sūta Saṁhitā* is one such teaching. In the Vedāntic tradition, it is believed that Śrī Śaṅkara studied the *Sūta Saṁhitā* eighteen times before composing the *Brahma Sūtra Bhāṣya*. This testifies to the greatness of the *Sūta Saṁhitā*.

तामष्टादशधाऽऽलोक्य शंकरस्सूतसंहिताम् ।
चक्रे शारीरकं भाष्यं सर्ववेदांतनिर्णयम् ।।

tāmaṣṭādaśadhālokya śaṅkarassūtasaṁhitām ।
cakre śārīrakaṁ bhāṣyaṁ sarvavedāntanirṇayam ।।

Śrī Śaṅkara studied the *Sūta Saṁhitā* eighteen times before he embarked upon his commentary on the *Brahma Sūtra*s. This commentary sets out all aspects of Vedānta in clear terms.

I personally feel that Śrī Śaṅkara composed the *Dakṣiṇāmūrti Stotram* after completing the *Brahma Sūtra Bhāṣya*. The *Sūta Saṁhitā* describes the incarnation of Dakṣiṇāmūrti in the following verses:

प्रलंबितजटाबद्धं चंद्ररेखावतंसकम् ।
नीलग्रीवं शरच्चंद्रचंद्रिकाभिर्विराजितम् ।।

गोक्षीरधवलाकारं चंद्रबिंबसमाननम् ।
सुस्मितं सुप्रसन्नं च स्वात्मतत्त्वैकसंस्थितम् ।।

गंगाधरं शिवं शांतं लसत्केयूरमंडितम् ।
वीरासने समासीनं वेदयज्ञोपवीतिनम् ।।

सर्वेषां प्राणिनामात्माज्ञानापस्मारपृष्ठतः ।
विन्यस्तचरणं सम्यग् ज्ञानमुद्राधरं हरम् ।।

स्वात्मभूतपरानंदपरशक्त्यर्धविग्रहम् ।
मुनिभिस्संवृतं मायावटमूलाश्रितं शुभम् ।।

ईशानं सर्वविद्यानामीश्वरेश्वरमव्ययम् ।
स्वात्मविद्याप्रदानेन सदा संसारमोचकम् ।।

दक्षिणामूर्तिदेवाख्यं जगत्सर्गादिकारणम् ।
रुद्र यत्ते मुखं तेन दक्षिणं पाहि मामिति ।।

पुनर्देवो महादेवो दक्षिणामूर्तिरीश्वरः ।
प्रदत्त्वा स्वात्मविज्ञानं तस्मै विप्राय सुव्रताः ।।

बहवो दक्षिणामूर्तिप्रसादादेव जंतवः ।
अनायासेन संसाराद्विमुक्ताः परमर्षयः ।। — मुक्तिखंडः, ४

pralambitajaṭābaddhaṁ candrarekhāvataṁsakam ।
nīlagrīvaṁ śaraccandracandrikābhirvirājitam ।।

gokṣīradhavalākāraṁ candrabiṁbasamānanam ।
susmitaṁ suprasannaṁ ca svātmatattvaika-saṁsthitam ।।

gaṅgādharaṁ śivaṁ śāntaṁ lasatkeyūramaṇḍitam ।
vīrāsane samāsīnaṁ vedayajñopavītinam ।।

sarveṣām prāṇināmātmājñānāpasmārapṛṣṭhataḥ ।
vinyastacaraṇaṁ samyag jñānamudrādharaṁ haram ।।

svātmabhūtaparānandaparaśaktyardhavigraham ।
munibhissaṁvṛtaṁ māyāvaṭamūlāśritaṁ śubham ॥

īśānaṁ sarvavidyānāmīśvareśvaramavyayam ।
svātmavidyāpradānena sadā saṁsāramocakam ॥

dakṣiṇāmūrtidevākhyaṁ jagatsargādikāraṇam ।
rudra yatte mukhaṁ tena dakṣiṇaṁ pāhi māmiti ॥

punardevo mahādevo dakṣiṇāmūrtirīśvaraḥ ।
pradattvā svātmavijñānaṁ tasmai viprāya suvratāḥ ॥

bahavo dakṣiṇāmūrtiprasādādeva jantavaḥ ।
anāyāsena saṁsārādvimuktāḥ paramarṣayaḥ ॥
— *Muktikhaṇḍaḥ*, 4

He has tied down his matted hair. He has adorned the head with the crescent moon. His neck has blue hue. He is shining brilliantly in the light of the autumnal moon. He is calm and smiling, being established in his own *ātman*. He holds Gaṅgā on his head. He is all-auspicious and serene. He is adorned with bracelets on the upper arms. He sits comfortably in *vīrāsana*, a yogic posture. His sacred thread represents the Vedic knowledge. The ignorance of *ātman* of all beings, in the form of the demon Apasmāra, is held under check below his feet. He removes the ignorance of the devotees with the fingers of the hand held in *jñāna-mudrā*, a specific configuration signifying the essential identity of *jīva* and *Īśvara*. His body is half-woman, the woman being his own Supreme power of infinite happiness, not different from Himself. *Dharma* in the form of a bull is besides him. The sages who live a life of *dharma* (righteousness) and who are well versed in the Vedic knowledge are all around him. He is sitting under the banyan tree, which stands for the *Māyā*. He is

> the repository of all branches of knowledge. He is the Lord of lords, immutable. He relieves the devotees from the clutches of *saṁsāra* by giving them knowledge about their own *ātman*. This Lord of creation, sustenance and annihilation is known by the name of Dakṣiṇāmūrti. The devotee prays to Him thus: 'O Rudra (one who drives away sorrow)! You are facing south. Please protect me'. Praying thus, the devotee worshipped the Lord again and again. O sages of severe austerities! The Lord Dakṣiṇāmūrti, greatest among all the celestials, bestowed upon that brāhmaṇa devotee the knowledge of *ātman*. O great sages! Many *jīva*s gained liberation from *saṁsāra* easily by the grace of Lord Dakṣiṇāmūrti.

Apasmāra, the inability of the mind to grasp the higher truths, is metaphorically presented as a demon, who is kept alive but, of course, under the right foot (control) of the Lord Dakṣiṇāmūrti. In the *Gītā*, Lord Śrī Kṛṣṇa declares that memory, knowledge, and forgetfulness are all caused by Himself (who is present in the heart of the *jīva* as the awareness, *ātman*).

> मत्तस्स्मृतिर्ज्ञानमपोहनं च । (१५-१५)
> *mattassmṛtirjñānamapohanaṁ ca* । (15-15)

This *apohana* is Apasmāra. Lord Dakṣiṇāmūrti shows *cin-mudrā* in His right hand. His is Ardhanārīśvara *svarūpa*, one half male and the other half female, the latter being none other than His *Māyā Śakti*. There is an ear-ring in the left ear of Dakṣiṇāmūrti, indicating the female nature of the left half. The right half is *Īśvara*, and a snake serves as a ring in the right ear. He is the cause of the universe (and also of its sustenance and dissolution). His seat is under the banyan tree, which stands for His creative faculty, the *Māyā*

Śakti. Sanaka, Sanandana, Sanātana and Sanatkumāra are the four disciples receiving knowledge from Him.

Propitiation of guru

It is well known that the configuration of the nine planets has an important bearing on the events in the life of a person. Among these nine planets, Jupiter (the planet *guru*) occupies an important place and influences the life of the person in a big way, especially the knowledge-based life of the person. Generally, we propitiate *guru* not only when he is in an unfavourable position, but also when one or more of the other planets are unfavourable, since *guru* influences the effects of other planets also. The best way to propitiate the planet *guru* is to visit the temple of Dakṣiṇāmūrti and recite this encomium, since *guru* as a planet is related to knowledge in the life of the person, and these verses contain the supreme knowledge presented in the form of an encomium. Thus, recitation of these verses is one of the best methods for warding off the ill effects of the planets in general, and of the planet *guru* in particular, in one's life.

Before you try to know *Īśvara*, you need to know yourself correctly, and for this you need the help of *guru*. I asked a person, 'Who are you?' Pat came the reply : 'I am Subbarao'. Subbarao is a name. You are not Subbarao. When somebody says 'I am Subbarao', he has completely identified himself with a name. The person was very much there before the naming ceremony (*nāmakaraṇa*). Even now, his wife calls him by another name. Name is meant for easy reference only. The jail authorities give a number to the prisoner. Address of a person is nothing more than the address of the body. Are you the body? Or is the body yours? You are the in-dweller of the body. Body is an object of your understanding. Bhagavān says in the *Gītā*:

देहिनोऽस्मिन् यथा देहे कौमारं यौवनं जरा ।
तथा देहांतरप्राप्तिर्धीरस्तत्र न मुह्यति ।। (२-१३)

dehinosmin yathā dehe kaumāraṁ yauvanaṁ jarā ।
tathā dehāntaraprāptirdhīrastatra na muhyati ।।
(2-13)

Just as for an individual there is in this body childhood, youth and old age, so too is the gaining of another body. With reference to that, a wise person does not come to grief.

The idea is that you should know yourself. There is no hurry to know *Īśvara*. At first, know yourself correctly. That knowledge is the panacea for all troubles. You are that. Your essential nature is called *ātman*. Here Śrī Śaṅkara is praising the glory of *ātman* in the form of Dakṣiṇāmūrti. This *stotra* is an encomium of *ātman* as much as that of *Īśvara*. The glory of *ātman* and that of *Īśvara* are merged in it. Sureśvarācārya, one of the four direct disciples of Śrī Śaṅkara, wrote a commentary (called *vārttika*) on *Dakṣiṇāmūrti Stotram* in verse form. The name of this commentary is *Mānasollāsa*. Therein, Śrī Sureśvara introduces this special aspect of the *stotra* in the following introductory verses:

आत्मलाभात्परो लाभो नास्तीति कवयो विदुः ।
तल्लाभार्थं कविस्स्तौति स्वात्मानं परमेश्वरम् ।। (१-२)

ātmalābhātparo lābho nāstīti kavayo viduḥ ।
tallābhārthaṁ kavisstauti svātmānaṁ parame-śvaram ।। (1-2)

That there is no gain superior to that of *ātman* is known to the wise. For the purpose of gaining the knowledge of *ātman*, the poet here is praising the glory of the Supreme Lord who abides in the form of his own *ātman*.

स्वेच्छया सृष्टमाविश्य विश्वं यो मनसि स्थितः ।
स्तोत्रेण स्तूयतेऽनेन स एव परमेश्वरः ।। (१-३)

svecchayā sr̥ṣṭamāviśya viśvaṁ yo manasi sthitaḥ ।
stotreṇa stūyate'nena sa eva parameśvaraḥ ।। (1-3)

The Supreme Lord created this universe by his own will. Having created it, He entered into it obtaining in the mind. That Lord in the form of *ātman* alone is glorified in this encomium by the poet.

Śrī Śaṅkara created monumental and voluminous three-tier literature of Vedānta (*Prasthānatraya Bhāṣya*s). *Prasthāna* means march towards the Supreme goal which is the knowledge of *ātman*. *Upaniṣad Bhāṣya*, *Brahmasūtra Bhāṣya* and *Gītā Bhāṣya* are the three *prasthāna*s, the express-ways taking the seeker to the highest Reality that is *ātman*. They constitute the first level of Vedāntic literature. Then come the *prakaraṇa* texts or treatises like *pañcīkaraṇam*, *tattvabodha*, *vākyavr̥tti*, etc. They are like the bye-lanes merging into the express-way. Everyone of them deals with one special topic of Vedānta and thus a student becomes familiar with the basic tenets of Vedānta by studying a few of these *prakaraṇa*s before starting the more serious study of *prasthāna*s. Śrī Śaṅkara is the teacher *par excellence* of Vedānta, and this is brought out vividly in the large number of *prakaraṇa* texts authored by him.

There is the third level of Vedāntic literature, comprising various *stotra*s sung by Śaṅkara from time to time praising the glory of *Īśvara*. My effort to eulogise *Īśvara* is like the effort of a child to describe the ocean. Even the best description of the ocean falls short of its real glory. This part of the literature is extremely useful for *saguṇa upāsanā*, worship of *Īśvara* in a particular aspect. One should correctly understand the basis of *stotra* literature and *saguṇa* worship.

We cannot say that one variety of *pūjā* is superior to another. All modes of worship are equally valid and efficient. *Īśvara* understands all types of prayers and responds accordingly. In theory, *Īśvara* has infinite forms and infinite names that go with them. This is how we have so many *sahasra nāma*s and countless *stotra*s. This is possible because He is essentially without name and form. The grand journey towards *Īśvara* indeed starts with a given name and a form. However, it so happens that people get stuck at the level of name and form. In Sanskrit, name is called *nāmadheyam*, which means *nāmamātrameva*, just a name. Name is not the essential content or reality. For an ornament, its essential content is gold; not its name, not form. People often ask a question: What is *Māyā*? The simplest answer to this profound question is: *Māyā* is name and form. One should gradually rise to the appreciation of *svarūpa* (essential nature of *Īśvara*). If you insist that *Īśvara* has one particular form, he becomes one more object, one more person, and thus becomes vulnerable in some degree or the other to all the problems that an individual like you and me face. We should know that *Īśvara* is the *mūla dhātu*, the basic content or reality of all that is, all that exists.

Human being is essentially a conscious being. His essential nature, namely, knowledge, has no particular form. Suppose the knowledge, which a person is, were to have a particular form. Then knowledge of that form alone takes place, to the exclusion of every other form. If the form of a pot is fixed to the knowledge, only pot-knowledge takes place. No other *jñāna* will take place. Fortunately the situation is not so. I am essentially awareness. When I see a pot, I become aware of the pot; next moment, the pot-form of the awareness is replaced by another form. Thus, I become aware of all forms, while essentially remaining formless awareness. What is the form of flour? Is *pūrī* the form of flour? No. Since flour has no form of its own, we can make *capātī* out of it, *pūrī* out of it or any kind of dish out of it.

Existence Absolute, 'is' is also formless like even awareness. Hence, many forms can be superimposed on it. It can be a pot. Pot 'is' or cloth 'is'. Sun 'is'. Moon 'is'. Atom 'is'. Electron 'is'. Thus Existence Absolute, the 'is-ness' has no particular form, and so it manifests as many forms. And that 'is-ness' (Existence) and that knowledge are one and the same (*sat* and *cit*). Once you understand the essential *svarūpa* of *Īśvara*, any form can be superimposed on it. All forms become a value addition. Any form can be fun. Suppose the Lord comes in the form of Śrī Kṛṣṇa; I take pleasure in it and worship him. Suppose He comes in the form of Śiva; I equally enjoy and worship Him. He comes in the form of a beggar, an ant; I still enjoy. One may not be stuck with any particular form, except may be in the initial stages of *sādhanā*.

There is a general feeling that *saguṇa Brahman* (the Lord with a form) is easy to understand and easy to contemplate. I say *nirguṇa Brahman* is easy to understand and better for contemplation. *Saguṇa Brahman* is a superimposition on the *nirguṇa nirviśeṣa caitanya* (the attribute-less form-less awareness), which is *Parameśvara*. *Dakṣiṇāmūrti Stotram* sings the glory of such *nirguṇa nirākāra parameśvara*. The compound word Dakṣiṇāmūrti can be split in the *karmadhāraya* (descriptive) as well as *bahuvrīhi* modes as follows:

दक्षिणश्चासौ अमूर्तिश्च दक्षिणामूर्तिः ।
दक्षिणाभिमुखा मूर्तिः यस्य सः दक्षिणामूर्तिः ।।

dakṣiṇaścāsau amūrtiśca dakṣiṇāmūrtiḥ ।
dakṣiṇābhimukhā mūrtiḥ yasya saḥ dakṣiṇāmūrtiḥ ।।

He is *amūrti*, without a particular form, which is same as saying that he alone manifests in all forms. *Dakṣiṇaḥ* means *samarthaḥ*, capable. He is in charge of creation, sustenance and annihilation of the entire universe. He is the almighty. He is the *adhiṣṭhāna* (substratum or locus) for the entire creation. In the second mode of splitting the compound word, it means the Lord facing the south. The Lord in the incarnation of a Teacher is facing the south such that the students face the north. This is an ideal arrangement. Facing the south means facing death. While learning Vedānta, the students should face the north. During sleep, you should not keep your head towards the north. The north stands for knowledge and immortality. Mṛtyuñjaya, the Lord who conquers death, resides in the north. The south stands for mortality (*mṛtyu*). Gaṅgā originates in the north and from there flows towards south. Man's life originates from *ātman*, which is *Īśvara*.

As one wakes up from sleep, the mind becomes active and the very first thought is 'I am' (*aham asmi*), which is the only reality about an individual. Later arises the thought 'I am the body in the world', which is ignorance and the beginning of *saṁsāra*. The north stands for *ātman*, and the south for *saṁsāra*. In Vedānta, *mṛtyu* (death) does not mean physical death, because there is nothing like the death of the physical body, which never lived, while *ātman* never dies. In the *Vivekacūḍāmaṇi*, it is described that *pramāda*, inadvertence or indifference and forgetfulness towards the truth is the real *mṛtyu*.

प्रमादो ब्रह्मनिष्ठायां न कर्तव्यः कदाचन ।
प्रमादो मृत्युरित्याह भगवान् ब्रह्मणस्सुतः ।। (३२२)

pramādo brahmaniṣṭhāyāṁ na kartavyaḥ kadācana ।
pramādo mṛtyurityāha bhagavān brahmaṇassutaḥ ।।
(322)

One should never be slothful about abiding in the *ātman* which is *Brahman*. Slothfulness is indeed the death, said the revered sage Sanatkumāra, the son of the Creator.

This indifference is a product of ignorance. Normally individuals live in ignorance, and the flow of life is towards the south; that is, the person engrossed in the *saṁsāra* is indifferent towards the knowledge of *ātman*; being identified with the body, he is travelling fast to embrace the waiting death. We should reverse this flow of life going in the wrong direction. We should start looking towards the north. We should strive to know our true nature. Also, the general tendency of the human beings is wordliness or looking outward. This attitude of looking outwards is to be arrested and one should develop an attitude of looking inwards. Looking outwards amounts to subject-object division, which is the real *saṁsāra*. The message is that there should be a change in the direction of life in general. Gaṅgā reverses its direction of flow towards the north at Kāśī (Benāres or Vārāṇasī). That is why Kāśī became a holy and auspicious place. Thus, when the student faces the Lord and seeks knowledge, he has turned his back on ignorance and now he is facing Dakṣiṇāmūrti, the embodiment of *ātma-jñāna*, and the flow of his life becomes as sacred as Gaṅgā in Kāśī.

Dakṣiṇāmūrti Stotram is a text of prayer by itself, but Śrī Śaṅkara starts it with another verse of prayer, because the text serves the dual purpose of prayer as well as teaching and any teaching has to be started with a prayer.

मौनव्याख्याप्रकटितपरब्रह्मतत्त्वं युवानं
वर्षिष्ठांतेवसदृषिगणैरावृतं ब्रह्मनिष्ठम् ।
आचार्येंद्रं करकलितचिन्मुद्रमानंदरूपं
स्वात्मारामं मुदितवदनं दक्षिणामूर्तिमीडे ।।

maunavyākhyāprakaṭitaparabrahmatattvaṁ yuvānaṁ
varṣiṣṭhāntevasadṛṣigaṇairāvṛtaṁ brahmaniṣṭham ।
ācāryendraṁ karakalitacinmudramānandarūpaṁ
svātmārāmaṁ muditavadanaṁ dakṣiṇāmūrtimīḍe ॥

maunavyākhyāprakaṭitaparabrahmantattvaṁ — one who has disclosed the essential nature of *Para Brahman* by a silent exposition; *yuvānam* — young in age; *varṣiṣṭhāntevasadṛṣigaṇaiḥ* — by the elderly sages who were students; *āvṛtam* — surrounded; *brahmaniṣṭham* — one who abides in *Brahman*; *ācāryendram* — the foremost among the teachers; *karakalitacinmudram* — displaying *cin-mudrā* (a particular configuration of fingers) with the hand; *ānandarūpam* — one whose essential nature is happiness; *svātmārāmam* — one who enjoys his own nature which is happiness; *muditavadanam* — one whose face is joyous, *dakṣināmūrtim* — Lord Dakṣiṇāmurti; *īḍe* — I praise the glory of.

The young Lord Dakṣiṇāmūrti, abiding in *Brahman*, surrounded by groups of elderly sages who are his resident students, makes the essential nature of *Para Brahman* clear to them by a silent exposition. This foremost of the teachers shows the fingers of his hand in a particular configuration indicating the knowledge of the essential non-difference of *jīva* and *Īśvara*. I pray to the Lord who is the embodiment of happiness, abiding in his own essential nature that is happiness, and radiating it through His face.

In this verse, the poet wields the words as the colours and brush and draws a beautiful picture of the Lord before our mind's eye. Such a descriptive poem is called *śabda citram*, a picture drawn with words on the canvas of the mind of the reader. *Īḍe*, the last word of the verse, is the verb; it means 'I praise the glory of'. The object of praise is Dakṣiṇāmūrti. The rest of the words in the verse are predicates to the word Dakṣiṇāmūrti; they are nine in number.

The *devatā*s like Indra, etc., have attained exalted positions by virtue of their good *karma*s in the earlier life or lives. Indra is called Śatamakha, one who performed hundred *yajña*s. But that does not make him necessarily a *jñānī*, knower of *ātman*. *Jñāna* is not something to be attained at the level of *karma* or by *karma*. So, if even Indra wants to know *ātman*, he has to approach a teacher, since he is a limited being himself due to ignorance, though he happens to be the overlord of heavens. It is indeed described in the eighth chapter of *Chāndogya Upaniṣad* that Indra approaches the sage Kaśyapa for the knowledge of *ātman*; he studies with the great sage for hundred and one years, before he gains fulfilment.

The sages control their senses and mind and perform difficult penance. But, that will not give them liberation from the sense of being a limited individual. Even such great sages, in spite of their unparalleled penance, can still remain ignorant of *ātman*. They have to approach a *guru*. The well-known celestial sage Nārada is an embodiment of the *bhakti* (*upāsanā*). He is indeed the author of the *bhakti* aphorisms, well-known as *Nārada Bhakti Sūtras*. It is described in the *Chāndogya Upaniṣad* that he once approaches the sage Sanatkumāra to gain fulfilment through the knowledge of *ātman*, which was still eluding him, since Nārada came to know by hearsay that the knower of *ātman* crosses the ocean of *saṁsāra*.

तरति शोकमात्मवित् । (७-१-३)
tarati śokamātmavit । (7-1-3)

The venerable sage taught him *brahma-vidyā*. Thus, one may be well accomplished as a *karmī* or *upāsaka*; still one has to discover a student in himself and approach a *guru* for gaining the knowledge of *Brahman* or *ātman*. We should not think that our student-days are over, now that we are elders. We have to come out of such a mind-set and discover the student in us; that is the foremost qualification for the student of *brahma-vidyā*. In the present verse, it is described that such great and elderly sages were seated all around Dakṣiṇāmūrti seeking knowledge. In contrast to them all, the Lord himself is quite young (*yuvānam*). When it comes to knowledge, the age and gender do not matter. We may recollect the famous statement of the poet Bhavabhūti in his *Uttara-Rāma-Caritam*.

> गुणाः पूजास्थानं गुणिषु न च लिंगं न च वयः ।
> *guṇāḥ pūjāsthānaṁ guṇiṣu na ca liṅgaṁ na ca vayaḥ* ।
>
> People respect the virtuous for their good qualities; mere gender or age cannot command respect of others.

The Lord is elaborating the essential nature of *Brahman* through *mauna vyākhyā*, a unique process of teaching without uttering a word. Some people may construe this as some sort of mysticism. But in the field of knowledge, mysticism has no role to play. It is not a transmission of knowledge through a beam of rays. Such an interpretation is not acceptable. *Śakti* or energy may be transmitted this way; they call it *śaktipāta* in Yoga. But it has no significant role to play with reference to *jñāna*. Here we can interpret *mauna* this way: the Lord is teaching the final truth through body language, through the language of *mudrā*. Speech is normally used in teaching. But teaching of Vedānta is very unique. Here, the subject-matter, *ātman*, is not available for objectification. It is not available for knowing through perception or inference. Even *śabda* (the words) as a *pramāṇa* cannot directly reveal *ātman*. Every word spoken by us has its origin in a thought in the mind. The thought is nothing but a wave-like motion in the awareness, which is *ātman*. Thus mind is subtler than words, and, in turn, *ātman* is subtler than mind. Hence, the words and mind put together cannot objectify their source, which is *ātman*. This is mentioned in the *Taittirīya Upaniṣad* in so many words:

> यतो वाचो निवर्तंते । अप्राप्य मनसा सह ।। (२-४-१, २-९-१)
>
> *yato vāco nivartante* । *aprāpya manasā saha* ।। (2-4-1, 2 9-1)
>
> Words together with the mind tried to depict the *Brahman*, but failed.

The journey towards the *ātman* is entirely by negation and rejection. If *ātman* is separated from you in space, you have to think of a path, the time needed to travel, and the effort required. You have moved away from yourself. The journey to *ātman* consists of only negating all superimpositions that you have on *ātman*. The non-availability of *ātman* to any means of knowledge is highlighted by the word *mauna vyākhyā*.

Mauna vyākhyā can be understood differently: In the presence of the Teacher, the likes and dislikes, the other deep-rooted impressions, and even the ego of the disciple are suspended and the person is able to abide in his own *svarūpa*, the *ātman*, which is *Brahman*. As already mentioned, *Brahman* is not separated from oneself either in time or space. So, the only obstacle for the realisation of this truth is the mind with its multifarious projections and the ego. In the divine presence of Dakṣiṇāmūrti, these are automatically eliminated and the disciples, who are great sages and seers in their own right, could rightaway abide in the *Brahman*, which is *ātman*. Bhagavān Ramaṇa Maharṣi is a modern example for this kind of silent teaching.

Vyākhyā means a statement that reveals a meaning. Quite often these statements reveal the meaning directly, in which case, the meaning is called the primary meaning (*mukhya-artha*). Occasionally, we come across a statement, whose primary meaning is a self-contradiction; but, being a statement made by a wise man or even by the Veda, it cannot be meaningless. So, we have to look for the implied or secondary meaning (*lakṣya-artha*). This method of revealing a truth by implication, or indirectly through a statement is called *lakṣaṇa*. As already mentioned, the Veda cannot define *ātman*, but it can teach *ātman* through *lakṣaṇa*. Vedānta statements help the student to negate quite a few misconceptions about *ātman* that is *Brahman*; then, the background reality of all these misconceptions, namely, the self-evident *ātman*, alone remains as the *svarūpa* of the seeker. This kind of unique indirect teaching methodology is indicated by the word *mauna vyākhyā*. This is the third interpretation of this unique aspect of Lord Dakṣiṇāmūrti's teaching. I believe that this method is followed by psychiatrists in treating people suffering from psychological problems. Consider this dialogue between one such doctor and a patient.

Doctor: Sir, what is your problem?

Patient: I feel I am inferior to many around me.

Doctor: No; I do not find any reason to think so. On the other hand, on close scrutiny, it is clear to me that you are quite well-accomplished.

The doctor's treatment does not bring about any new embellishments to the personality of the patient. He just tries to eliminate a misconception that the patient developed about himself.

Ācāryendram: Lord Dakṣiṇāmūrti is the foremost among the teachers of *ātma-jñāna*. In *pravṛtti dharma*, the person expands without; he collects flowers, goes to the temple and performs *pūjā,* etc. The society is sustained in dynamic equilibrium by *pravṛtti dharma*. Sages like Marīci received this *dharma* from *Īśvara* in the form of Veda and carried it forward in the society. Because of this *dharma* alone, the creation marches forward. *Nivṛtti dharma* consists of closing the window-like sense-organs, thus shutting off the world. Then the seeker, as though, goes within (*antarmukha*) and abides in his own essential nature which is *ānanda*. This is called *ātma-niṣṭhā/brahma-niṣṭhā/jñāna-niṣṭhā*. This is presented as the means of liberation in the following verse of *Kaṭhopaniṣad*:

परांचि खानि व्यतृणत्स्वयंभूस्तस्मात्पराङ् पश्यति नांतरात्मन् ।
कश्चिद्धीरः प्रत्यगात्मानमैक्षदावृत्तचक्षुरमृतत्वमिच्छन् ।। (२-१-१)

parāñcikhāni vyatṛṇatsvayambhūstasmātparāṅ
paśyati nāntarātman ।
kaściddhīraḥ pratyagātmānamaikṣadāvṛtta-cakṣu-
ramṛtatvamicchan ॥ (2-1-1)

The Lord created the sense organs in such a way that they are always outward-looking and thus He destroyed them. This is the reason why human beings are normally outward-looking and lack the inward disposition. But there arises in the multitude of people somebody, desiring immortality, who reverses this disposition and directs it towards his own innermost reality and comes to know the Supreme reality which is his own Self.

Bhagavān in the *Gītā* mentions, among many things, two values related to this *niṣṭhā*.

> विविक्तदेशसेवित्वमरतिर्जनसंसदि । (१३-१०)
>
> *viviktadeśasevitvamaratirjanasaṁsadi* । (13-10)
>
> The disposition of repairing to a quiet place; no longing for the company of the people.

The Lord, the embodiment of happiness that is essentially natural (*ānandamūrti*), is described as abiding in this *brahma-niṣṭhā*. Lord Śiva is described in the Purāṇas as doing penance. What is the object of his meditation? It cannot be anything other than Himself, because He Himself is the Supreme Lord. The Lord or the knower of *Brahman* is ever happy with Himself, in Himself, by Himself; nay, He is indeed the happiness crystallised (*svātmārāmam*). No surprise that His face radiates that inner happiness (*mudita vadanam*). *Jñānī* is happy for no particular reason. His happiness is not dictated by the outside circumstances. The sages Sanaka, Sanandana, etc., were the original students of this *ātma-dharma*. From whom did they learn? From Dakṣiṇāmūrti, who is the embodiment of *ātma-dharma*. He is the knowledge. Knowledge is his *svarūpa*. Knowledge and happiness go together.

The *Taittirīya Upaniṣad* defines *Brahman* by implication as:

> सत्यं ज्ञानमनंतं ब्रह्म । (२-१)
>
> *satyaṁ jñānamanantaṁ brahma* । (2-1)
>
> The Existence Absolute, which is the infinite, and which is also the awareness, is itself *Brahman*.

Ananta means *pūrṇa*, complete without a second. This *pūrṇatva* is not different from *ānanda*. In fact, whenever we gain happiness, in that moment, we are the whole.

First Verse

Now, let us take up the first verse of the *Dakṣiṇāmūrti Stotram*.

विश्वं दर्पणदृश्यमाननगरीतुल्यं निजांतर्गतं
पश्यन्नात्मनि मायया बहिरिवोद्भूतं यथा निद्रया ।
यस्साक्षात्कुरुते प्रबोधसमये स्वात्मानमेवाद्वयं
तस्मै श्रीगुरुमूर्तये नम इदं श्रीदक्षिणामूर्तये ।। १ ।।

viśvaṁ darpaṇadṛśyamānanagarītulyaṁ nijāntar-gataṁ
paśyannātmani māyayā bahirivodbhūtaṁ yathā nidrayā ।
yassākṣātkurute prabodhasamaye svātmāname-vādvayaṁ
tasmai śrīgurumūrtaye nama idaṁ śrīdakṣiṇā-mūrtaye ॥ 1 ॥

विश्वं (*viśvaṁ*) — universe, दर्पणदृश्यमाननगरीतुल्यं (*darpaṇa-dṛśyamānanagarītulyaṁ*) — equivalent to a city seen in a mirror, निजांतर्गतं (*nijāntargataṁ*) — included within oneself, आत्मनि (*ātmani*) — in the Self, मायया (*māyayā*) — by virtue of ignorance, यथा निद्रया (*yathā nidrayā*) — like even by sleep (in the dream), बहि उदभूतं इव (*bahiḥ udbhūtaṁ iva*) — as if created outside, पश्यन् (*paśyan*) — seeing, यः (*yaḥ*) — whosoever, प्रबोधसमये (*prabodhasamaye*) — at the time of waking up or gaining knowledge, अद्वयं (*advayaṁ*) — non-dual, स्वात्मानं (*svātmānaṁ*) — one's own self, साक्षात्कुरुते (*sākṣātkurute*) — discovers, तस्मै (*tasmai*) — unto that, श्रीगुरुमूर्तये (*śrīgurumūrtaye*) — who is in the form of the revered teacher, श्रीदक्षिणामूर्तये (*śrīdakṣiṇāmūrtaye*) — unto Lord Dakṣiṇāmūrti, इदं (*idaṁ*) — this, नमः (*namaḥ*) — obeisance.

The universe, like even the city being seen in the mirror, is within oneself. But, just as in sleep, one sees the world as though it is created outside, while all along it remains on the substratum of one's own *ātman*. Whosoever realises his own non-dual *ātman* on gaining knowledge, is indeed the same as the Lord Dakṣiṇāmūrti, who is in the form of the Teacher. This is my prostration unto Him.

Let us first take up the last line of the verse since it is repeated in every verse, except the very last. *Namaḥ*, prostration is an expression of humility on the part of the devotee. Humility is the single most important quality of a true student. Our scriptures proclaim that knowledge and humility go together.

विद्या ददाति विनयम् ।
vidyā dadāti vinayam ।

Knowledge gives humility.

Even Bhagavān in the *Gītā* clubs both of these qualities together, indicating their inseparable nature.

विद्याविनयसंपन्ने ब्राह्मणे . . . (४-१८)
vidyāvinayasampanne brāhmaṇe . . . (4-18)

The knower of *Brahman* endowed with wisdom and humility. . . .

Namaḥ means 'nothing is mine'.

न मे (न मम) इति नमः ।

na me (na mama) iti namaḥ ।

We develop a lot of attachment to objects, situations and people. This attachment to the things outside, as though, binds us to them. The basis for such an attachment is nothing but delusion. Attachment has no basis in logic or truth. Even the origin of gravitational attraction between two bodies, which is physical in nature, is not completely understood. What to speak of a purely subjective attraction between me and the things outside? This truth is recognised when I say *namaḥ* before *Īśvara*. Everything that I consider me and mine (body-mind-sense complex) is given to me without exception and the giver is called *Īśvara*. In recognition of this truth I bow my head before *Īśvara* (*namaḥ*) and understand 'not mine' as 'not mine'.

Two gentlemen are fighting over a piece of land. The Goddess of Earth (*Pṛthvī*) laughs at their folly. She mutters to herself:

> Your parents, grand-parents, great grand-parents were having similar attachment to me. They have all disappeared. Now you are quarrelling over me? You will soon perish. I will remain the same, unaffected by your false attachment.

We see the politicians fighting over the waters of rivers. This is sheer folly. *Namaḥ* means recognition of this truth and surrendering the attachment to the things of the world at the feet of the Lord.

The phrase *na mama* (not mine) is continuously repeated in a Vedic ritual at the end of every oblation. The *na mama* of the Vedic ritual appears as *namaḥ* in the *Stotram*. The seeker of knowledge prays: O Lord, everything including my body-mind-sense complex belongs to you. When that is so, where from this ego (*aham* and *mama*) has come? Śrī Śaṅkara in his *Brahma Sūtra Bhāṣya* (*Adhyāsa Bhāṣya*) says:

> मिथ्याऽज्ञाननिमित्तस्सत्यानृते मिथुनीकृत्य अहमिदं ममेदमिति नैसर्गिकोऽयं लोकव्यवहारः ।
>
> *mithyā'jñānanimittassatyānṛte mithunīkṛtya ahamidaṁ mamedamiti naisargiko'yaṁ lokavyavahāraḥ* ।
>
> The human interaction consisting of the very natural notions, 'this is me' and 'this is mine' has its origin in ignorance which is false, because of which, the human being mixes up the Truth with the falsehood.

In every chant of '*namaḥ* unto *Īśvara*' uttered with feeling, this ignorance gets negated. In the *Mahābhārata*, it is said that the word *mama* (mine) is death.

> ममेति द्व्यक्षरो मृत्युः ॥
> *mameti dvyakṣaro mṛtyuḥ* ॥
>
> The word of two syllables, *mama*, is indeed the death.

In the *saṅkalpa* of a Vedic ritual or *pūjā*, we hear the word *mama*. Normally people say only *mama* and the rest is said by the priest. I suggest that we should not say *mama* alone; it should be said in association with the entire phrase found in the *saṅkalpa*.

> ममोपात्तदुरितक्षयद्वारा श्रीपरमेश्वरप्रीत्यर्थम् ।
> *mamopāttaduritakṣayadvārā śrīparameśvara prītyartham* ।
>
> By eliminating the omissions and commissions on my part and thus gaining the grace of the Lord.

Gurumūrtaye. *Mūrti* means a form. *Satyanārāyāṇamūrti* —

the form of the Lord obtaining in Annavaram of Andhra Pradesh is a manifestation of Satyanārāyāṇa. The Lord can be in any form. In the incarnation of Dakṣiṇāmūrti, he is in the form of a *guru*, the universal teacher of the universal truth. In the context of a student approaching the teacher for the knowledge of *ātman*, he should visualise the Lord Dakṣiṇāmūrti in the teacher before him. This *gurumūrti* is once again essentially non-different from the seeker, who is referred to by the pronoun *tasmai* in the last line of the verse. Thus we have a statement of prayer which at once negates the apparent difference between *Īśvara*, *guru* and the seeker. This spirit is beautifully captured by Sureśvarācārya in his *Mānasollāsa*.

> ईश्वरो गुरुरात्मेति मूर्तिभेदविभागिने ।
> व्योमवद्व्याप्तदेहाय दक्षिणामूर्तये नमः ।। (१-३०)
>
> *īśvaro gururātmeti mūrtibhedavibhāgine* ।
> *vyomavadvyāptadehāya dakṣiṇāmūrtaye namaḥ* ।।
> (1-30)
>
> My prostrations unto the Lord Dakṣiṇāmūrti, who is all-pervading like even the space, and who manifests in the different forms of the Lord, the Teacher and the Person.

The non-dual reality can appear as manifold because it reflects in different *upādhi*s (limiting adjuncts). The technical word *upādhi* means a thing which appears to transfer its own qualities to another thing simply by juxtaposition; the other is called *upahita*. We should keep in mind that the attributes of the *upādhi* are not really transferred to the *upahita*; that *upahita* only seems to have acquired the properties of *upādhi*. For example, when a red flower is placed by the side of a pure crystal, the latter appears red. The flower is called the *upādhi* for the crystal which is *upahita*. Space is all-pervasive. But the needle-space appears to be different from the all-pervasive space and also appears to be limited; the limitation of the needle being superimposed on the space itself. Similarly, in the incarnations of Rāma etc., the person is the *upādhi* of *Īśvara*. Sun is the *vibhūti* or *upādhi* through which *Īśvara* is shining. In the present context, the all-pervading Lord appears severally through the three *upādhi*s as *Īśvara*, *guru*, and *ātman*. There is no *vastu bheda* (essential difference) among them. You take yourself to be small and insignificant only because you take the limitations of the *upādhi*, the body, on yourself due to ignorance of your real nature, the *ātman*, which is none other than the Lord.

The word *guru* is quite often misused. People address any unknown person like an auto-driver, bus-conductor, etc., as *guru*. Such an address on the part of a person indicates at once that there is no preceptor in the life of that person, which is very unfortuante. Some people take the priest who helps them to conduct certain rituals like *pūjā* etc., as *guru*. Some other people take the astrologer who fixes the auspicious time (*muhūrtta*) for a marriage, etc., as *guru*. These ideas about *guru* are wrong. Even the person who initiated the seeker into a *mantra* can be taken as *guru* only in a secondary sense. Primarily such a person can only be called *mantropadeṣṭā*. In a primary sense, the word *guru* means the preceptor who taught the *mahāvākya*, the great statement, which helps the seeker to understand the essential non-difference between *ātman* and *Brahman*. *Gu* means *ajñāna*, ignorance; *ru* means one who removes it. Thus, *guru* is that teacher who removes my ignorance of *ātman*, that is, myself.

The first three *pāda*s of this verse describe the nature of *ātman*, which is none other than you. *Viśvam* means the world of plurality. We normally take this world as pluralistic as well as independent of me, the observer. This world-view, born of ignorance, betrays lack of intelligent analysis on our part. The world is not independent of me; it is indeed very much connected with me; dependent upon me. *Viśvam* is something that you hear (*śabda*), you see (*rūpa*), you smell (*gandha*), you taste (*rasa*), and you touch (*sparśa*). The world consists of just these five sense-objects, *viṣaya*s. What is the connection between this *viśvam* and me? The general notion is that I am an isolated being and hence insignificant, one more object in this plurality of things called *viśvam*. This notion is false. 'I am' — we are sure only of this. Any thing you add to 'I am' . . . we are not sure of that. I know 'I am'. I don't need others to tell me that 'I am'. I am self-evident. I am the awareful presence. *Jagat* also is there. Does it exist outside of me, independent of me? No. The world is in me, swallowed by me (*nijāntargataṁ*). *Viśvam* is included in me. *Ātma-sattā* (existence of *ātman*, or better, the existence that is *ātman*) includes *jagat-sattā*. This is a bold and profound statement, almost bordering on outrageous.

Necklace and bracelet are different only as ornaments, but, in terms of the metal out of which they were made, they are one and the same. Take the example of space (*ākāśa*). Is it manifold? It appears to be so; like needle-space, pot-space, room-space, hall-space, etc. But space is partless and hence undivided and indivisible. But, due to the limiting adjuncts, it looks as though divided. Similarly, when we say 'pot is', we are talking of the existence conditioned by the pot. When we say, 'the cloth is', again we are talking of the same existence, but as though limited by another limiting adjunct called cloth. Thus there is one undivided, indivisible Existence Absolute (*akhaṇḍa-sattā*), which is *Īśvara*, that is, *ātman*.

Viśvam is nothing more than what is perceived through the five sense-organs and conceptualised by the intellect. Beyond that there is no *viśvam*. My world consists of my likes and dislikes. They are different from yours. My friend is my friend. Do you consider him as your friend? He is unknown to you; you consider him as another person. The response in my mind towards him is that he is my friend. Where is the friend? In the mind. Is the son inside or outside? He is inside; outside there is a human being. I say outside there is a living being, or even better, a being, which evokes the response of son in you. Thus, our friends, foes and all relations are only in the mind; which, in turn, has its existence in the infinite awareness, that is, *ātman*.

It may be argued that though the relationships based on subjective interpretation may be inside, but the objects of the world are very much outside and are commonly perceived as such by all. This seemingly perfect argument is wrong from the standpoint of the Supreme Reality. Take the example of a flower. When I say that I see the flower, I am not perceiving the existence called flower; I am only seeing the colour and the form of that existence. Eyes do not see the Matter, the *vastu*; they see colour and form alone. Existence as such is not available for perception. Colour is not an intrinsic property of the flower. The reflected rays of light from the so-called 'flower' fall upon the retina after they are focussed by the eye-lens. The optic nervous system connected to the retina gets activated in the form of electric sensations. These sensations are conveyed to the brain through the nervous system and the brain has got a software of *saṁskāra*s. A child sees something but does not see a flower till the mother prevails upon it a dozen times saying that it is a flower. That is why only the person who knows the flower can see it.

The forms and names are already recorded in the mind in the form of *saṁskāra*s. A Tarzan brought up in the forest will not be able to see many common things, that the people in the society outside see and take them for granted as such, since his mind does not have the *saṁskāra*s of a so-called civilised society. A computer not loaded with the software cannot answer the questions of that nature. Colour is the response of the mind to the reflected rays of light from this matter. Therefore, what you have before is the *vastu* and the rays of light that are reflected are interpreted by the mind as colour and form, which are instantly associated with the name 'flower'.

Let us do an experiment to prove that the flower is not outside but within you, so that we can thereby establish that the whole world is included in you. Let me remove petal after petal, while all the time asking you the question: Is this a flower? Each time the answer is 'no'. Finally, is this stalk the flower? No. Is this group of petals and stalk the flower? No. When two things are put together, in whatever way they may be arranged, they do not amount to a new, a third thing. They do not become a third object. They continue to be the same two objects, unless there is a chemical reaction between the two to form a new compound. Therefore, many 'non-flowers' put together do not constitute a flower. It simply continues to be a combination of 'non-flowers'. Combination is not a distinct entity. A combination is just a combination only. Here, the *tārkika*s, the Indian logicians, say that the combination of 'non-flowers' constitutes a flower. But this contention is obviously incorrect, since any combination of 'non-flowers' cannot be a new object called flower. They maintain that a particular combination has the special property of flower-ness associated with it. What is this 'flower-ness'? It is the property of being the flower, they say. You can clearly see the fallacy of mutual dependance (*anyonya-āśraya-doṣa*) in this argument. It is like saying that Subba Rao's house is next to Rama Rao's house. Where is Rama

Rao's house? Rama Rao's house is next to Subba Rao's house.

Vedānta rescues this situation; flower is nothing but a *rūpa*, a mental concept. There is no flower outside the concept called flower. The concept itself is evoked by an outer thing. Thus, there is a contribution from the thing, which is outside with reference to the body. However, along with the concept of outside, the concept of flower indeed has its existence in the mind, which in turn depends upon the awareness, that is *ātman*, for its existence.

Flower is an interpretation by the mind of the *vastu*, which appears to be outside from the body's point of view. There is no flower outside the concept of the flower. What is a concept? Concept is a thought frame (*vr̥tti*), like a picture appearing in a movie, which is nothing but a succession of film frames. *Vr̥tti* is a thought frame. Mind undergoes a modification in the form of the flower. So, flower is nothing but flower-*vr̥tti*. Whatever objects you see, or even better, you think you are seeing, they are in the form of thought frames. Consider a wave that has arisen in the ocean. The wave has originated from the ocean. As long as it lasts, where does it exist? It exists in the ocean itself. It cannot walk away from the ocean onto the shore. When it dies away, it goes back into the ocean. Wave is nothing but particularisation of that infinite water-body. Wave is nothing but water. Similarly, flower is a thought frame, which is none other than the mind with a particular modification. The thought frame is born from the ocean of consciousness, which is the bedrock or matrix of the mind. That infinite awareness, *ātman*, includes the entire world of objects perceived and conceptualised.

You do not smell the flower. You smell the fragrance of the flower. Fragrance is an interpretation of a sensation in the mind. A few molecules of a very volatile liquid chemical present within the flower spread in the air due to volatility. A few of the molecules enter into the nose. Nose is a sense-organ. It has the capacity to recognise a particular molecular structure. The nose membrane has a receptor site, which recognises this molecule. The molecule goes and sits on the receptor. The nerve endings recognise the molecule by virtue of an enzymic reaction and the resulting nerve sensations are transmitted to the mind. The mind analyses these sensations against an already existing reference code (a scent code). Hence the mind recognises it, say, as a rose. What you know through nose is the *gandha* (smell), which is a *guṇa*, quality. Similarly *rūpa* (colour and form) is a quality; *rasa* (taste) is a quality. You perceive the qualities; not the *vastu* itself. *Vastu* is not available for perception. So the flower is a concept of the mind (a mental flower). Only that person who has a *saṁskāra* of the flower in him can see the flower. Just as I see Mona Lisa in the computer printout in an IBM advertisement.

I remeber an advertisement that I have seen recently in the *New York Times*. It was a digital computer printout consisting of rows and columns of 0's and 1's. But there is a contrast in the densities of these numbers from one square inch of the paper to the other square inch. Because of that contrast, I could clearly recognise the figure of Mona Lisa in it. A person who does not know Mona Lisa cannot see Mona Lisa in it, though he may recognise a human face. On the other hand, a living being that does not have an idea of human form cannot recognise a human form in it. Is Mona Lisa inside or outside? Mona Lisa is inside. This is what is meant by *viśvam nijāntargatam*.

Thus, this world of our experience is nothing more than name and form, *nāma* and *rūpa*. Are they inside or they are outside the mind? They are not entirely outside. It is a subjective interpretation of what is outside. Outside there is *vastu*, which acquires a plurality due to *Māyā Śakti*, the creative or manifesting faculty of *Īśvara*. As long as the *ātman* is wrongly limited to the body, that is, as long as there is identification with the body, there exists a world outside with reference to a line running close to the body. If this false boundary is obliterated in the wake of the knowledge of the all-pervading *ātman* which is *Brahman*, then the division of subject and object vanishes, and the essential unity of both in the infinite awareness is realised. Thus, the world of names and forms has its existence entirely in the mind, and with reference to the non-dual Awareness, that is *ātman*, the subject-object division resolves in that infinite awareful Existence Absolute. We assume we have a body and a mind and inside there is *ātman*. This is false. From this wrong perspective I look at the world. The world appears to be the one against me and outside of me. The world is outside; so also is the body. Both of them are in the Awareness of the Witness. Only when you identify yourself with the body, the world appears to be outside of you. For a selfish person, only the body is his *ātman*; even the family members are not included in his *ātman*. For the mature people, their *ātman* includes the family. If you do any harm to my wife or son, it harms me, because they are included in my *ātman*. If you take this expansion of the I-ness to its logical conclusion, which is the all-pervading *ātman*, then the whole world is included in the *ātman*. *Viśvam nijāntargatam*. Sureśvarācārya explains this expansion of I-ness to *Brahman* in a beautiful verse.

भुक्तं यथान्नं कुक्षिस्थं स्वात्मत्वेनैव पश्यति ।
पूर्णाहंताकवलितं विश्वं योगीश्वरस्तथा ।।

— *मानसोल्लासः*, १-१५

bhuktaṁ yathānnaṁ kukṣisthaṁ svātmatvenaiva paśyati ।
pūrṇāhantākavalitaṁ viśvaṁ yogīśvarastathā ॥
— *Mānasollāsaḥ,* 1-15

The food in the plate is viewed as different from me; but after eating, it is considered an integral part of me. Similarly, the great *jñānī*'s I-ness is so complete that it can swallow (include) the entire universe into itself.

What is the dance that appears on the cinema screen? It is nothing but a series of film frames in motion. The matrix of that dance is the light thrown by the projector on the films. The varying intensity of the light emanating from the films in quick succession appears as dance on the screen. In the same way, this universe is like a movie on the screen of mind and the light that illuminates it is the Infinite Awareness, the *ātman*. Thus the entire *jagat* has its existence in *ātman*. There is nothing like a purely objective world. The world is subjective. It is the projection of the mind. Hence the world is not outside; it exists in *ātma-caitanya*. The body exists in the *ātman*. The mind exists in the *ātman*. The Upanīṣads declare the same truth again and again:

इदं सर्वं यदयमात्मा । — बृहदारण्यकोपनिषत्, २-४-६
idaṁ sarvaṁ yadayamātmā ।
— *Bṛhadāraṇyakopaniṣat*, 2 4-6

Whatever is here is all *ātman*.

Vedānta is a vision which is given here and now. If you understand this, your *saṁsāra* drops off. Vedānta is not a belief system. Here, Śrī Śaṅkara brings in the dream-model to further illustrate the vision that the universe exists in *ātman*. Yesterday night, I had a dream. In the dream, I went to Australia, and from there to Saylorsburg, USA. I taught there for a length of time and then returned to India. All the things of the dream, including the teacher, the student, the fundamental subject-object division, the living and non-living, the moving and non-moving, appear as if they are outside of me, the dreamer. Are they really outside of me? I was looking at them in the dream as though they were outside of me. This is a trick played by the dream on me in the sleep. Where were the mountains in the dream? In me. Where was the teaching in the dream? In me. Where was the concept of outside? In me. This is what I say once I wake up from the dream. Somehow the dream created a difference, where the difference never existed. The subject (me, the dreamer) in the dream was *ātman*. All the objects of the dream were also essentially *ātman*.

There is no such experience in which the object is present, but the subject is absent; or vice versa. As long as a pot is present, the knower of the pot is also present. Pot-knowledge does not exist independent of 'I know the pot'. *Draṣṭā* (the knower) and *dṛśya* (the known) come into existence simultaneously when I wake up from sleep and disappear simultaneously when I go back to sleep. Thus they emerge out of the same source of consciousness and resolve into the same source. That consciousness is *ātman*.

There is another such sleep called *ajñāna-nidrā*, as described in *Mānasollāsa*.

अनादिमायया सुप्तो यदा जीवः प्रबुध्यते ।
अजमनिद्रमस्वप्नमद्वैतं बुध्यते तदा ।। (१-१३)

anādimāyayā supto yadā jīvaḥ prabudhyate ।
ajamanidramasvapnamadvaitaṁ budhyate tadā ।।
(1-13)

> The *jīva* (individual soul) is asleep (ignorant) due to the beginningless *Māyā*. When he becomes awake (by knowledge), he realises the non-dual *ātman*, which transcends the three states of waking, dream and sleep.

In the dream we see the unreal subject-object division. We should note that the subject-object division is not the issue. But the reality of this division is the issue. All the divisions in the dream as well as in the waking state can be reduced to the fundamental subject-object division. This is the universal experience. When you come out of the dream, the entire dream world of subject-object division is resolved into the essential nature of the dreamer. Similarly, when the seeker exposes his intellect to the light of teaching of *Śāstra*, he comes out of this dream of world experiences, which is caused by the beginningless *Māyā,* or *ajñāna*. Then, the subject, the limited 'I' and the objects merge into the non-dual *ātman*, like even two jets of water sprouting out of a fountain due to a force merge into the fountain itself when the force is withdrawn. That *ātman* happens to be you. That is the teaching of Dakṣiṇāmūrti. Dakṣiṇāmūrti does not exist outside that non-dual *ātman*. Therefore, *tasmai śrīgurumūrtaye nama idaṁ śrīdakṣiṇāmūrtaye*.

Second Verse

In the first verse *tvam padārtha* (the reality of the *jīva* or individual) has been analysed. Now, the second verse deals with the nature of *Īśvara vis-a-vis jagat*, the universe (*tat padārtha*). For example, the *tvam padārtha* is analysed in the first set of six chapters of the *Gītā*, *tat padārtha* in the second set, and finally *asi padārtha*, the essential non-difference between *tat* and *tvam* in the third set. This completes the analysis of the *mahāvākya*, *tat-tvam-asi*, which is the essence of all the Upaniṣads. Here is the second verse:

बीजस्यांतरिवांकुरो जगदिदं प्राङ्निर्विकल्पं पुनः
मायाकल्पितदेशकालकलनावैचित्र्यचित्रीकृतम् ।
मायावीव विजृंभयत्यपि महायोगीव यस्स्वेच्छया
तस्मै श्रीगुरुमूर्तये नम इदं श्रीदक्षिणामूर्तये ।। २ ।।

bījasyāntarivāṅkuro jagadidaṁ prāṅnirvikalpaṁ punaḥ
māyākalpitadeśakālakalanāvaicitryacitrīkṛtam ।
māyāvīva vijṛmbhayatyapi mahāyogīva yassvecchayā
tasmai śrīgurumūrtaye nama idaṁ śrīdakṣiṇāmūrtaye ॥ 2 ॥

बीजस्य (*bījasya*) — of the seed; अंतः (*antaḥ*) — inside; अंकुरः इव (*aṅkuraḥ iva*) — like even the sprout; इदम् (*idam*) — this; जगत् (*jagat*) — the universe; प्राक् (*prāk*) — earlier to; निर्विकल्पम् (*nirvikalpam*) — without any divisions; पुनः (*punaḥ*) — again at the time of creation, मायाकल्पितदेशकालकलनावैचित्र्यचित्रीकृतम् (*māyākalpitadeśakāla-*

kalanāvaicitryacitrīkr̥tam) — the universe of wondrous plurality was made by relation to space and time brought about by *māyā*; यः (*yaḥ*) — who, मायावी इव (*māyāvī iva*) — like even a magician; अपि (*api*) — and; महायोगी इव (*mahāyogī iva*) — like a great *yogī*, स्वेच्छया (*svecchayā*) — with his own volition; विजृंभयति (*vijr̥mbhayati*) — presents with great fanfare, तस्मै श्रीगुरुमूर्तये नम इदं श्रीदक्षिणामूर्तये (*tasmai śrīgurumūrtaye nama idaṁ śrīdakṣiṇāmūrtaye*).

Like even the sprout inside the seed, this universe before creation was the unmanifest *Brahman*. Then afterwards, *Māyā* has brought in a relationship for that unmanifest with time-space, thereby creating the universe of wondrous plurality. That *Īśvara* (*Brahman* from the standpoint of creation), like even a magician or a great *yogī*, creates this universe by his own will. My prostrations unto that *Īśvara*, who has taken the incarnation of the universal teacher, Śrī Dakṣiṇāmūrti.

Normally, people have some rudimentary understanding of the *tvam* and *tat*. But, this knowledge is sullied by a lot of misinformation. This situation has to be set right. It is called *śodhana*. Philosophers of ancient India pondered over the subject of creation with an open mind, and came out with very ingenious theories about the origin of the universe. A correct understanding of the origin of the universe is tantamount to the correct understanding of *Īśvara*. At first, let us examine a few of these theories, while analysing the present verse.

Theories of creation

All theologies begin their efforts to understand the unknown, namely, the God in heaven, and then try to understand the known, namely, the universe before us as an appendage to that God. Such a journey starting from the unknown is possible only in a faith or belief-based system. This is the reason why the theology based religions are called faiths. But, in Vedānta, as in science, we try to understand the unknown by starting our analysis with the known world, since the unknown, being the origin of the known is a universal fact. In Vedānta, we do not accept that *Īśvara* has created this universe by a miracle. If we say creation is literally a miracle of *Īśvara*, no effort is put in understanding the creation.

Jagat is available to us as an object of our perception, inference, etc. Based on what we can know of the universe with the help of these two basic *pramāṇa*s (means of knowledge), namely, perception and inference, we can easily appreciate that this universe is an effect, since everything within it including the planets, stars and galaxies are effects (*kārya*) bound by time. Every object in this universe is a *kārya*. The human being is also a *kārya*, a combination of various types of cells, from the point of view of the body. Every object is a *kārya* intelligently put together. The universe, as a collection of many objects in space, is also very intelligently put together. Science is the result of the efforts to understand the intelligence behind all the objects of the universe. The behaviour of everyone of these objects follows a set of natural laws. The planets revolve round the sun in specified orbits with specific angular velocities. Even the sun, the stars, and the galaxies obey natural laws. There is nothing in this universe which can be described as random or disorderly. Even the random events are amenable to a statistical order. Even the disorder of the universe follows an order as characterised by entropy studies. Therefore, it is easy to conclude that the universe must have an intelligent cause, *cetana kāraṇa*. *Brahman*, Bhagavān, *Parameśvara*, and *Īśvara* are some of the names used to refer to that cause.

Cosmologists 1: Steady State Theory

We have a branch of modern science called cosmology. There was a school of thought in cosmology, called Steady State Theory. The universe that we know now is like this from times immemorial and it will continue to be like this forever. A few planets may die, and in their place new planets may emerge. A few stars may die and in their place new stars may be born, and so is the case with the galaxies. It is our experience that every day a few people die and their place is taken by new arrivals. The human race continues uninterrupted, in spite of some superficial changes. In the same way, universe was and continues to be more or less the same. There was nothing like a beginning and no original creation. Based on the same line of thinking, there will be no end to the universe also. This Steady State Theory was propounded by Fred Hoyle. The *mīmāṁsaka*s of ancient Indian philosophy were the original exponents of this Steady State Theory. They maintained that this universe was and will be, never different from what it is now.

न कदाचिदनीदृशं जगत् ।

nakadācidanīdṛśaṁ jagat ।

The universe was never different from what it is now.

Because of this view, the *mīmāṁsaka*s have no use for the creator. Among the *vaidika*s (the followers of Vedic authority), the earlier *mīmāṁsaka*s are called *nirīśvaravādin*s, though the latter day *mīmāṁsakas* accepted *Īśvara*. It is significant to note that ancient sages like Jaimini who lived about two thousand years ago had the vision to anticipate this Steady State Theory, much before the present-day cosmologists.

Cosmologists 2: Big-Bang Theory

The scientists of the Bell Laboratories discovered a background microwave radiation spreading throughout the space, indicating that an enormous explosion took place in the distant past. The radiation of that explosion travelled all this time in space and it has now reached here. By analysing that radiation we can know a few things about that explosion. We can see the birth of a star that was born a few years ago now in the telescope, since the light takes that many years to reach us from that star. Thus we see the universe of the past through these radiations. The universe was created in the distant past in a phenomenon called Big Bang. Before the creation took place, this universe was in the form of a huge ball of energy of infinite density with very high temperatures. That massive ball of undefined energy exploded with a big-bang and the resultant cooling effect caused the enormous energy of the ball to coalesce into gaseous clouds, which have further cooled into galaxies and stars. The radiation emanating from that enormous explosion is spread all around in the universe and can be seen now in the microwave region. The discovery of this background radiation of the Big Bang spreading throughout the cosmos effectively put an end to the Steady State Theory.

Śūnyavādins

There is a school of thought among Buddhists who maintain that the universe has originated from *śūnya*, the void. It is the general experience that there are two causes behind every effect.

1. *Nimitta kāraṇa*, the efficient cause: A sentient being, like the pot-maker takes a decision to create an object, procures the raw materials, works for it and makes the creation of the pot possible.

2. *Upādāna kāraṇa*, material cause: For example, the clay out of which the pot is made.

The *śūnyavādin*s do not accept a *nimitta kāraṇa* for the *jagat*. They take the awareness as an epiphenomenon of the matter and the matter itself to have originated from *śūnya* or void; that is, the universe is a superimposition by the mind on void.

This contention is untenable. How can an existent thing originate from void? This view is opposed to the *śruti*, *smṛti* and logic.

कथमसतस्सज्जायेत । — *छांदोग्योपनिषद्*, ६-२-२

kathamasatassajjāyeta — *Chāndogyopaniṣad*, 6-2-2

How can an existing thing arise from non-existence?

नासतो विद्यते भावो नाभावो विद्यते सतः ।
उभयोरपि दृष्टोऽन्तस्त्वनयोस्तत्त्वदर्शिभिः ॥
— *श्रीमद्भगवद्गीता*, २-१६

nāsato vidyate bhāvo nābhāvo vidyate sataḥ ।
ubhayorapi dṛṣṭo'ntastvanayostattvadarśibhiḥ ॥
— *Śrīmadbhagavad-Gītā*, 2-16

For the unreal, there is never any being. For the real, there is never a non-being. The ultimate truth of both of them is seen by the knowers of the truth.

Sat, an existent thing continues to be *sat*. *Asat,* unreal continues to be *asat*. *Sat* and *asat* are mutually exclusive. One cannot become the other. Light is light and darkness is darkness. The objects of the universe are understood as existing. When we say pot, we mean 'pot is'. This 'is-ness', which is associated with every object of the universe, must also be associated with the cause, since the cause pervades the effect; and the cause and the effect cannot possess two mutually exclusive properties. A marvellous refutation of the *śūnyavāda* is found in the *Kaṭhopaniṣad*:

अस्तीत्येवोपलब्धव्यस्तत्त्वभावेन चोभयोः ।
अस्तीत्येवोपलब्धस्य तत्त्वभावः प्रसीदति ।। (२-३-१३)

astītyevopalabdhavyastattvabhāvena cobhayoḥ ।
astītyevopalabdhasya tattvabhāvaḥ prasīdati ।। (2-3-13)

We should know that *ātman* 'is' and that *ātman* is the limitless existence that transcends the ideas of 'is' and 'is not'. Among these two, for the one who has understood *ātman* as the 'is' of the objects of the universe, the unconditioned Existence Absolute becomes well appreciated.

Anything you understand is understood as something that is existing. For example, *ghaṭaḥ asti*, *paṭaḥ asti*, *śatruḥ asti*, *mitram asti* (pot is, cloth is, enemy is, friend is). Then how could a thing which is understood as *asti* (is) originate from the void? *Śūnya* cannot be the cause of the universe.

Tārkikas and Vaiśeṣikas

Kaṇāda is the originator of the system of Indian logic. His name signifies his preoccupation with atoms. *Kaṇa* means atom. Kaṇāda means one who eats atoms. *Īśvara* is the efficient cause of the universe; he creates the universe out of atoms, which are the material cause. Where from these atoms have come? They are as permanent as *Īśvara* is. Thus they have a reality which is equal to that of *Īśvara*. The *jagat*, which is made up of those atoms, has the same reality as that of *Īśvara*. This school of thought is also called *asatkāryavāda*, since they maintain that the *jagat*, which was non-existent, came into existence, due to the agency of *Īśvara*. There is an elaborate rebuttal of this view in the *Brahma Sūtra Bhāṣya* of Śrī Śaṅkara.

Sāṅkhya system

The Sāṅkhya system of philosophy contends that the universe has originated from the original material cause called *pradhāna* by transformation. *Pradhāna* is obviously insentient, as the material cause is supposed to be. This theory is called *satkāryavāda*, in contrast to the *asatkāryavāda* of the Vaiśeṣikas, since the Sāṅkhyas maintain that the effect is present in a latent form in the cause. Sāṅkhyas do not accept *Īśvara*; they maintain that *pradhāna* transforms itself into the universe, due to a disturbance in its constituents, which are the three *guṇa*s, *sattva*, *rajas* and *tamas*. It is like the clay becoming a pot on its own. This theory obviously fails to account for the reason why the insentient *pradhāna* should, on its own, undergo transformation in the first place. This system is elaborately refuted by Śrī Śaṅkara in his *Bhāṣya*s.

Vedānta

In the *Taittirīya Upaniṣad*, an young man Bhṛgu approaches the teacher, who happens to be his own father, and asks him to teach *Brahman*.

> अधीहि भगवो ब्रह्मेति । — *तैत्तिरीयोपनिषत्*, ३-१
>
> *adhīhi bhagavo brahmeti* । — *Taittirīyopaniṣat*, 3-1
>
> O revered teacher! please teach me *Brahman*.

The teacher replies thus:

> यतो वा इमानि भूतानि जायंते । येन जातानि जीवंति । यत्प्रयंत्यभिसंविशंति । तद्विजिज्ञासस्व । तद्ब्रह्मेति ।।
>
> *yato vā imāni bhūtāni jāyante* । *yena jātāni jīvanti* । *yatprayantyabhisaṁviśanti* । *tadvijijñāsasva* । *tadbrahmeti* ।।

From what indeed all these beings take birth; having taken birth, they live (exist) by virtue of what; and in the end they get merged into and become one with what; desire to know That. That is *Brahman*.

The teacher advises the student to know *Brahman* by inquiry and investigation. He also gives a few hints about the nature of inquiry to be conducted. This universe has originated from *Brahman*. That is the first indicator. From this, we can understand that *Brahman* is the cause of the universe, but it is not clear whether *Brahman* is both a material cause and an efficient cause. Then the teacher says that the universe exists in *Brahman* itself. This gives us a hint of things to come. *Brahman* might be the material cause also, in addition to being the efficient cause. Otherwise, how does one explain the existence of the universe in *Brahman*? The third sentence confirms this hint. The universe resolves into the *Brahman*. That clearly shows that *Brahman* is the material as well as the efficient cause rolled into one. This is indeed a revolutionary idea, like the Law of mass-energy equivalence of Einstein. This vision of *Īśvara* being the material-cum-efficient cause of the universe is unique to Hindu philosophy. Such a revolutionary vision is not found in other schools of thought in the entire world. This definition of *Brahman* is summarised in the famous *Brahma Sūtra*:

जन्माद्यस्य यतः । (१-१-२)

janmādyasya yataḥ । (1-1-2)

That is *Brahman*, from which the creation etc., of this universe take place.

Vivartavāda

Some thinkers propose that this universe has originated by transformation of *Īśvara*. This transformational causation is not tenable on many counts:

(i) If *Īśvara* were to transform into the universe, then as of now there would be no *Īśvara* since he must have been exhausted in the process; like, as pots are being produced, the clay is used up. Or worse still, *Īśvara* would have a huge wound in himself, since a part of him is transformed into the universe.

(ii) *Īśvara* would be a material with parts, since that is the essential condition for transformation to become possible. Transformation is nothing but a change in configuration of certain parts. In such a situation, *Īśvara* will be transient, like every other aspect of this universe and must disintegrate sooner or later.

(iii) *Īśvara* would be bound by time, since all transformations proceed in time. But, we are talking about the origin of the universe including space and time.

(iv) Transformational causation is possible only in the insentient; not in a conscious being. Consciousness is the witness of all transformations.

This untenable situation is wonderfully remedied by the concept of *Māyā*. Vedānta visualises that the universe is an apparition (*vivarta*) in *Brahman*. Here, it may be pointed out that *abhinna-nimitta-upādāna-kāraṇatva* (the status of being the material-cum-efficient cause) is possible only as an apparition. If I have to make a pot, I need clay. But, if I have to visualise a pot, like in a dream, I do not need any material except 'myself', the consciousness, in which anything and everything is visualised. Thus, this universe is seen in the Supreme Reality, the *Brahman*, not made out of *Brahman* or something else. Thus, the creation is nothing but manifestation of names and forms out of the unmanifest

Brahman. Names and forms are just apparent; not real.

Let us take the example of embroidery, which is a self-design. A picture of a landscape consisting of a mountain, the sun rising from behind the mountain peaks, a river flowing by the mountain, a boat in it, and a boatman and a cow on the bank standing by the side of a tree are all there in the woollen embroidery. On the tree there is also a bird. All these things of the landscape — the Sun God, the mountain and the river as the representatives of the Mother Nature, the tree (a sentient non-moving entity), the bird, the animal, the human being and the insentient boat — all came out of the ball of wool. Now, suppose we hold the knot of the embroidery and slowly pull it out. Then, what happens? Slowly, one after another, the entire landscape resolves into the ball of wool. When it existed, it did so in the wool. The matrix of the entire landscape with all of its plurality is none other than the ball of wool. The relationship of this universe with the creator is best exemplified by this. Bhagavān is that ball of wool while the embroidery is the universe. The essential reality of this universe is the *ātman*, which is *Brahman*.

The first line of the verse refutes the *śūnyavāda* and *asatkāryavāda*. *Nirvikalpa* means the unmanifest *Brahman* which possesses the creative (manifesting) faculty called *Māyā Śakti*, which is like the code of this universe in a potential form. This *Māyā Śakti* manifests into the many (*savikalpa*). Śrī Śaṅkara gives the example of the tree originating from the seed. The seed has the genetic code of the roots, trunk, branches, leaves, flowers and fruits, etc., of the tree within itself. In favourable conditions, that potential manifests as the different parts of the tree.

Look at the seed. It is just a featureless shell and kernel. The potential of the seed is not available for perception, whereas the tree can be seen, touched, tasted, smelt and its sounds can be heard. *Kārya* is always gross, while the *kāraṇa* is subtle. Seed is *nirvikalpa*, while the tree is *savikalpa*. We should not forget that the *nirvikalpa* seed and the *savikalpa* tree are both superimpositions on the five great elements, or even better, on the Existence Absolute, which is *ātman*. At the *kāraṇa* level, the emphasis is on the Reality (*vastu*), while at the level of *kārya*, the unreal name and form are highlighted. In the cause there is no plurality; it is not there even in *kārya*, which only appears to be plural, because the mind is deluded by name and form. The diversity is the property of *nāma-rūpa*. In the *vastu*, there is no diversity; it is the unity in and through the diversity. Thus, the substratum of *jagat* is the non-dual *Brahman,* which is the Existence Absolute appearing as many limited existences.

Māyā kalpita deśa kāla kalanā vaicitryacitrīkṛtam. The *jagat* is variegated with a plethora of names and forms. It is related to its substratum, the *Brahman*, like even the rope-snake is related to the rope. It appears on the locus of *Brahman* entirely due to the time-space framework created by *Māyā*, the creative faculty of *Brahman*.

Reality of nāma-rūpa

According to Newton, the objects, which can be considered as mass points (entire mass of the object appearing to be fixed to the centre of gravity), are moving in absolute space and absolute time. These motions follow certain laws. These are the famous Newton's laws of motion. The philosopher Descartes postulated that the Newtonian world of objects moving in space and time is not possible without an external architect. This architect is called God. The theologian's model of the universe is close to this Newton-Descartes model, except that Newton had the honesty of taking time and space into account and assuming them to be absolute, whereas the theologian either does not remember the inconvenient time and space in formulating his theory, or just conveniently ignores them.

According to Einstein, time and space are relative. Einstein is the first person after Śrī Śaṅkara to understand time-space correctly. No concept of time is possible without the concept of space. Clock is not time. Clock is a dial with the numbers and hands. Time is not the property of the clock. As the mind recognises the successive movements of the hands of a clock around a circular dial, it understands the succession of those events of motion as time, in accordance with a deep-rooted impression present in itself. There is sun, and there is a motion of the sun in the space (relative to earth). The movement of the sun across the horizon takes half-a-day. It is followed by a night. Night and day combined constitutes a whole day. That is how we measure time. If there were no space and no movement of the sun, there would be no time. The converse is also true. Plurality of objects is not possible without the concept of time and space. There is nothing like an object independent of time-space.

There is space, time and plurality of objects in the waking state. When you are in meditation or when you go to sleep, do you experience time, space and objects? No. All of them rise together in the mind and disappear together with the mind. All these three inter-dependent aspects put together constitute what is called *jagat.* A theologian presents *Īśvara* as external to the universe. What is it that separates *Īśvara* from *jagat*? Space does not separate *jagat* from *Īśvara,* because *jagat* itself includes space. We cannot say an object separates *jagat* from *Īśvara*, in which case *Īśvara* becomes one more object subject to decay and death. Time cannot be the separating factor between the *jagat* and *Īśvara,* because time is a part and parcel of the universe. There is no separating factor between *Īśvara* and *jagat*. This intrinsic relationship between the *jagat* and *Īśvara* (the superimposed and the locus of superimposition respectively) is beautifully presented in the *antaryāmī* brāhmaṇa of the *Bṛhadāraṇyaka Upaniṣad*. *Īśvara*, the creator of the universe, is very much present in this universe, in every particle of this universe and in every micro-second of the time as *antaryāmī*, the innermost reality. It is the glory of Vedic vision that it talks of an *Īśvara* who is not different from the *jagat* before us, and who is the only reality of this universe of plurality. Our mind is accustomed to recognise *nāma* and *rūpa* and in the process we miss the underlying truth. We have to shift our focus of attention from the *nāma-rūpa* to recognise the Truth. Vedānta looks at universal errors and not at individual errors. *Nāma-rūpa* is one such universal error.

You continue to commit the error, unless it is corrected. We look at a thing, see its form and give it a name and we forget the reality underlying the form and the name. Name and form are the projections of the mind. Why does the mind not look at the reality instead of projecting name and form? What is wrong with the mind? If we understand the working of mind, we can examine the elaborate process of correcting that mind.

Necklace is an ornament only when you wear it on the neck as an ornament. When you keep it in a locker, it is no longer an ornament. In the locker, it is just an article worth certain amount of money. When you remember it that you have to wear it in a party, it again becomes an ornament. In the banker's vision, it is a valuable, not an ornament. When you want to go to bed, it is not an ornament. It is an unwanted nuisance. It is an ornament only in terms of the specific projection of the mind. *Nāma-rūpa*, the ornament, is not the intrinsic property of the object. The concept of ornament is a superimposition on the reality.

Nāma-rūpa and time-space

The jewellery shop is a good example of *vaicitrya citrīkṛtam*. The variety of ornaments that we see in the jeweller's shop is purely a projection of the mind. The plurality of ornaments appears to be real, due to the mind's fixation, which is again the result of ignorance. The unreal appears to be real, and in the process we lose sight of the real.

The *saṁsāra* is in the mind and the method to overcome *saṁsāra* is also in the mind. Mind not understood or to go along with the mind is *saṁsāra*. By knowing the working of the mind, you can conquer the mind. You do not have to do anything more than knowing. You can only know the working of the mind through the mind itself. You cannot bring in the solution from outside. Teaching is not an outside solution. It is an intrinsic solution. Teaching helps you to see the truth for yourself and thereby correct yourself.

I want to connect *nāma-rūpa* to *deśa-kāla*. We have to consider an example with a smaller time-scale to appreciate the unreal nature of *nāma-rūpa*. Take the example of a wave. I saw a placid lake; then due to some disturbance, waves appeared in it. It is nothing but water during the presence as well as during the absence of waves. Let me put my hand in the wave. What happens? Will a piece of wave stick to my hand? No. The hand is wetted by water. What is the *ātman* (the essential reality) of the wave? Water. Wave is nothing but a form with a name. Where from *nāma* and *rūpa* have come? *Deśa kāla kalanā vaicitrya citrīkṛtam. Kalanā* means connection. *Citrīkṛtam* is *nāma-rūpa*.

Insert the wave-form in the framework of space and time axes. In the case of a wave the space is nothing but the amplitude of the wave, which is just a few centimeters for the small wave, and a few meters for huge waves. At 0'th sec, the amplitude of the wave is zero. Suppose the wave has a life span of one sec. At ½ second the wave reaches the highest point, the crest. In the first half second, the amplitude increases. In the second half second, the amplitude decreases. Thus the wave is a mental construct created by the time-space impressions that are in-built in the mind. It is nothing but water fixed into the framework of time and space. Take out the time-space framework. There was water before and there is water now. Knowing that, you can still enjoy the wave. Waves can also do a job of generating electricity. The person who sees waves as water, also sees *nāma* and *rūpa*. But he does not stop at the level of wave only. If it is so, it is called *sthūla dr̥ṣṭi* or *kārya dr̥ṣṭi*.

A peculiar thing about waves is that it looks as though there is a flow of water as the wave progresses. If you keep a cork on the wave, it does not move forward. It is only the wave that is progressing, or rather, appears to progress. The cork stays where it is. So the water is not moving but the wave is moving; it is *nāma-rūpa* that is moving. It is time-space that gives birth to name and form (*deśa kāla kalanā*). Science and Technology are concerned with *nāma-rūpa*. In an entire book of Wave Mechanics that I came across, there is not a single word about the substance of the wave even though various parameters such as wavelength etc., of the wave are discussed. The author is not interested in the substance of the wave. His interest is limited to only the mechanics of the wave. In Vedānta our concern is with the substance. The people in the world are engulfed in the mire of *nāma-rūpa* and develop a commitment to *nāma-rūpa*. This is *saṁsāra*. Once you are committed to something, you develop all logic to defend it. When you realise that *nāma-*

rūpa is *mithyā,* that it is only a shell, not the kernel, only then you can see the truth.

māyāvīva vijr̥mbhayatyapi mahāyogīva yassvecchayā ।

There is a wonderful model to understand the reality of the universe. The universe is nothing but the dance of *Īśvara*, the Naṭarāja. What is a dance? Dance implies a lot of knowledge. Every posture of the body in a dance sequence has significance. It is called *karaṇa.* I understand that there are 108 different *karaṇa*s. Every movement of the fingers, hands, feet, legs and other limbs of the body is associated with knowledge inherent in it. Dance is a manifestation of both *kriyā-śakti* (vital force) and *jñāna-śakti* (the power of knowledge). We find the wonderful expressions of both the energy and knowledge in our body. When I am talking, there is *kriyā-śakti* in the front supported by the *jñāna-śakti* from behind. The source from which both these powers originate is me, the *ātman.* The Sun God gives both heat and light. The Sun never sets; so also *ātman* never sleeps. The mind-stuff (*antaḥkaraṇa*) is the window through which the *ātman* shines. *Kriyā-śakti* is manifested through *karmendriya*s, the organs of action.

Is the dance, which is the manifestation of both vitality and knowledge, different from the dancer? No. No experience can exist outside the experiencer. It is the experiencer who imparts reality to the experience. It is the dancer whose awareful presence lends itself to the expression called dance. Dance remains as a potential in the dancer before he/she starts dancing. The person who is dancing is not just a dancer alone; he is a person in his own right. He is a dancer with respect to the dance. He is not intrinsically a dancer. The description of his potential as a dancer is only with respect to the dance, and that potential, being an expression of his innate nature, is not at all different from him, though we use the language of possessor-possessed.

Let us now come to *jagat*, which means 'one which is continuously on the move' (*gacchati iti jagat*). It is a dynamic universe both at macro- and micro-levels. It is the dance of the *Īśvara,* the Naṭarāja. This is the meaning behind the tradition of Naṭarāja-worship in the Hindu culture. The dance of Naṭarāja can be visualised in the perfect and orderly motion of particles in atoms and molecules, of the moon around the earth, of planets around the sun and also of galaxies in an ever-expanding universe. It can be felt in the body, in the flow of blood, in the beat of heart, in the digestion of food and in myriad physiological functions. The bodies of all living organisms are dynamic factories at work. The body's functions continue even when we sleep, because the Lord Naṭarāja, the *abhinna nimitta upādāna kāraṇa* of the universe, does not know sleep. Even an ant is a manifestation of *jñāna-śakti* and *kriyā-śakti*. The entire universe is a manifestation of *jñāna-śakti* and *kriyā-śakti.* Every motion in this creation is an orderly motion. Order implies knowledge. This *jñāna-śakti* and *kriyā-śakti* were there in *Īśvara* in an unmanifest form before creation. That unmanifest potential has a name. It is called *Māyā*.

The attributeless *Para Brahman,* in association with the creative potential is called *Īśvara,* or *saguṇa Brahman,* from the standpoint of this creation. Is the dancer and the person, one or two? They are one. Similarly *saguṇa Brahman* and *nirguṇa Brahman* are one. *Nirguṇa Brahman* is *satyam jñānam* and *anantam. Nirguṇa Brahman*, in association with *Māyā,* the creative faculty, is called *saguṇa Brahman*. This entire universe is none other than one *Īśvara* appearing as many. That *Īśvara* obviously includes me, the seeker too. It is only in ignorance that a seeker exists separate from *Īśvara*, the Lord Dakṣiṇāmūrti.

Third Verse

It has been established that *Brahman* is the apparitional cause of this universe in the second verse. Now, the relationship between the unreal plurality of the world and the Supreme Reality, the *Para Brahman*, is further elaborated in the third verse.

यस्यैव स्फुरणं सदात्मकमसत्कल्पार्थगं भासते
साक्षात्तत्त्वमसीति वेदवचसा यो बोधयत्याश्रितान् ।
यत्साक्षात्करणाद्भवेन्न पुनरावृत्तिर्भवांभोनिधौ
तस्मै श्रीगुरुमूर्तये नम इदं श्रीदक्षिणामूर्तये ।। ३ ।।

yasyaiva sphuraṇaṁ sadātmakamasatkalpārthagaṁ bhāsate
sākṣāttattvamasīti vedavacasā yo bodhayatyāśritān ।
yatsākṣātkaraṇādbhavenna punarāvr̥ttirbhavāṁ-bhonidhau
tasmai śrīgurumūrtaye nama idaṁ śrīdakṣiṇā-mūrtaye ॥ 3 ॥

यस्य इव (*yasya eva*) — of whom alone, स्फुरणं (*sphuraṇṁ*) — awareness, सदात्मकम् (*sadātmakam*) — which is essentially existence, असत्कल्पार्थगं (*asatkalpārthagaṁ*) — obtaining in the objects of unreal existence, भासते (*bhāsate*) — shining, यः (*yaḥ*) — who, साक्षात् (*sākṣāt*) — himself, तत् (*tat*) — that, त्वम् (*tvam*) — thou, असी (*asī*) — art, इति (*iti*) — thus, वेदवचसा (*vedavacasā*) — through the words of Vedas, अश्रितान् (*āśritān*) —

devotees, बोधयति (*bodhayati*) — teaches, यत् साक्षात्करणात (*yat-sākṣātkaraṇāt*) — by realisation of whom, भवांभोनिधौ (*bhavāṁbhonidhau*) — in the ocean of births and deaths, पुनरावृत्तिः (*punarāvṛttiḥ*) — returning back, न भवेत् (*na bhavet*) — does not happen, तस्मै श्रीगुरुमूर्तये नम इदं श्रीदक्षिणामूर्तये (*tasmai śrīgurumūrtaye nama idaṁ śrīdakṣiṇā-mūrtaye*).

The *Brahman*, which is Existence-Awareness Absolute, alone pervades all the objects of the world making them shine (making them evident), and imparting its own reality to them, which are themselves unreal. That *Brahman* is indeed you, the *ātman*. This is the teaching of the Lord in the form of the Vedas to his devotees. Whosoever realises this truth will not return to the ocean of repeated births and deaths. My prostrations unto that Lord Dakṣiṇāmūrti, who is in the form of the Teacher.

Sattā means existence. *Sphuraṇa* means becoming evident. These two terms are interconnected. A thing is validated as existing only when it becomes evident. A thing becomes evident because it exists. It is in the nature of the mind to divide where there is no division. The division as such is not the issue, but the reality of the division is. The presence is the awareness and the awareness is the presence. *Sattā* and *sphuraṇa* are two aspects of the same *vastu*. Seeing division where there is none is the cause of *saṁsāra*. The mind puts *sattā* (*asti*) outside and *sphuraṇa* (*bhāti*) inside. The criterion for this division is the false identification with the body. But *asti* and *bhāti* are one and the same, *sphuraṇaṁ sadātmakam*. Their unity in *ātman* can be recognised in meditation.

The words *jaḍa* and *cetana* are understood in different ways. Things having life are taken as *cetana* and lifeless objects as *jaḍa*. Sometimes, moving things are taken as *cetana* and unmoving as *jaḍa*. But in Vedānta, *jaḍa* is one which cannot know itself and cannot know others; whereas, *cetana* is one which knows itself and can know others. It is obvious that everything is known to me and I am self-evident.

You think that you are in the world. But the fact is that it is the world that is in you. You are the beacon of consciousness, the light that illuminates whatever comes in its way. Whatever is seen by you is *nāma-rūpa* superimposed on *sattā,* the Existence Absolute. The *sattā*, which is supposed to be outside, is indeed you, the awareness.

Asatkalpārthagaṁ bhāsate. It means that the existence, *sat*, appears as the unreal *nāma-rūpa*. Let us examine the statement: 'Pot is' (an existent pot). Existence is *viśeṣya*, substantive, and pot is *viśeṣaṇa*, an attribute. Pot was not there before; but 'clay is'. Pot is broken; but the 'broken piece is'. The one Being appears as an existent pot, as existent clay, and as an existent broken piece. *Ghaṭaḥ asti*, *paṭaḥ asti*, *mr̥t asti*, *rājā asti*, *sukham asti*, *duḥkham asti*. It is existence all through. One name ends; another name begins. One wave ends; a new wave begins. But water continues to remain and is unaffected. Getting engrossed in the name and the form is *saṁsāra*.

It is the existence that is primary and on that *nāma-rūpa* is superimposed. Thus, it is the Existence Absolute which pervades all objects of the world that are taken as existent. Also, this existence is awareness, since the pot does not exist outside the awareness of pot. Mountain does not exist outside the awareness of mountain. We look at the gold not as gold but as an ornament, which is the *upādhi* through which the reality, namely gold, expresses itself. Similarly, when the Reality expresses through the mind and senses, it is understood as *nāma-rūpa*.

There are objects and objects in this world. The Supreme Reality, *Param Brahman*, which is the cause of this universe, is not one more object. *Sattā* and *sphuraṇa* are the two aspects of the same Reality. *Sphuraṇa* means shining. It is not the light outside that lights up different objects. Even that light shines after the consciousness. That consciousness is you. The world exists because of you; because you bless it with your reality and your consciousness. Consider any particular human relationship. It exists because you bless it. Where is this relationship in sleep? Any object exists only when you impart reality to it. This is what is called *dṛṣṭi-sṛṣṭi-vāda*.

Sphuraṇa (becoming evident) is not the intrinsic property of the object. It is after your *sphuraṇa* that the object shines. The necklace exists because you see it. It means that if you stop seeing the necklace, it does not exist. When you decide to sell the necklace, you do not look at it as necklace. Then it is a valuable object which will bring in some urgent cash. When you see it as a necklace, it is a necklace. When you see it as a liquid asset, it is a liquid asset. When you see a person as son, he is a son. When you see a person as brother, he is a brother. When you see him as an enemy, he is an enemy. He is not an enemy at other times. There is no world other than your concept of the world. Are the objects making themselves known to you? Or is it you who are illuminating the objects of the world? You are like the miner with a headlamp illuminating the dark areas in the mine. Wherever the light of your consciousness falls, that particular area or object is illuminated. The world is a gallery and you are the central reality and the light because of which everything else exists and shines. If you have the knowledge of a particular branch of science, say physics, it is you the awareness in which that knowledge is shining. If there is ignorance in you, for example, you do not know the Russian language, it is once again the awareness, in the presence of which the ignorance is recognised.

Sattā-sphuraṇa is the essential reality of the universe. Name and form are only shadows. The substance of the wave is water. The substance of an ornament is gold. The substance of anything, which exists, is existence, which is the awareful *ātman*. The manifest has no independent reality. The essential content of the manifest is the unmanifest itself. Vedānta does not promise us the vision of Viṣṇu, Śiva, etc. It clears our misconceptions about reality. It tries to show that you are the very centre around which the whole universe is revolving in terms of reality, in terms of existence, in terms of getting known, and in terms of shining.

Sākṣāttattvamasīti vedavacasā yo bodhayatyāśritān. There are two types of statements. (1) *Jñāna-janya jñānabodhaka vākya* (2) *Jñāna-ajanya jñānabodhaka vākya.*

I see a pot. Immediately there is the knowledge of the pot, which is nothing but a form already known to me as such. This knowledge of form (*rūpa-jñāna*) gives rise to the knowledge of name, which is none other than the impression of the pot present in the mind from an earlier experience. Then, we say, this is a pot. This statement is the result of the knowledge of a given form. This kind of a *vākya* can never convey the ultimate truth, since it is entirely within the domain of sense-mind complex, which is the result of earlier impressions. The knowledge conveyed by this *vākya* is perceptual-conceptual knowledge. These *vākya*s are not going to lead one out of *saṁsāra* of *nāma* and *rūpa*.

The statements of the Veda are the products of the inspired vision of the sages (*jñāna-ajanya jñānabodhaka vākya*). It is the *Parameśvara,* who is all-knowledge, speaking through these sages. *Tat-tvam-asi* is one such *vākya*. It is not the result of perceptual-conceptual knowledge of a given person. In that sense, it is the impersonal knowledge revealed through a person of outstanding vision. In the present context, the Lord Dakṣiṇāmūrti gives this kind of knowledge of the oneness of *ātman* and *Brahman* (individual and *Īśvara*) to the students, who are great sages themselves.

Tat-tvam-asi. Take the example of a glowing incense stick. The glow is *agni*, which is one of the five great elements (*mahābhūta*s). It is the universal energy. The entire *jagat* is pervaded by it. That *mahāgni* is focussed in the glow of the incense stick. It is not born when the incense stick is lighted; nor it dies away when the stick is consumed by it. It is only the *upādhi*, the incense stick, which has birth and death. A small glow can consume a mountain of incense sticks. The smallness is with respect to the *upādhi* alone. There are no two fires; but there are two incense sticks. The size and plurality belong to the *upādhi*, not to the Reality. There is one vital energy (*prāṇa*) in all persons. The life of the person is entirely sustained by *prāṇa* or *vāyu*. You are the source of that *prāṇa*.

Mind is a bridge between *ātman* and body. Mind, identifying with its source, *ātman,* is *jīvanmukti* and the mind identifying with body is *saṁsāra*. We make a grievous mistake about ourselves. We identify ourselves with the body and thus get confined to the body. We consider the problems of the body as our own problems.

The entire universe can be reduced to two things: the knower (*draṣṭā*) and the known (*dṛśya*). You are that *draṣṭā*, the seer; to be more precise, you are the matrix of that seer (*dṛk-svarūpa*).

You have identified yourself with a false person, who is the creation of the mind. Mind in combination with ignorance becomes a person, Mr. So-and-so. We should note that Mr. So-and-so is not the subject, but is an object of the witnessing awareness. The person, who is a projection of the mind, is not intrinsic to you. Suppose somebody says that he is an attorney. If this status of being an attorney is understood as incidental, there is no problem. But, if that together with a few such other things constitutes the self-image, one becomes the prisoner of that image. In that person, the seen becomes the seer; and the seen engrosses and overwhelms the seer. This is ignorance; this is lack of discrimination. By falsifying the person by knowledge, there remains the *ātma-jyoti*, which is *Brahman*. If only you develop a detachment towards that person, Mr. So-and-so, and rise above the tyranny of the *ahaṅkāra*, then you are one with that Supreme Reality, which is all-shining, and which illumines the whole universe. This is the thesis of this verse.

As a result of this knowledge, the nucleus of an individual to which all actions and their results accrue, gets destroyed by the fire of knowledge. This resolution of the individual person in the *Brahman* is called *mokṣa*, the liberation. An individual, who dies an ignorant person, will take another birth in another body produced by the reservoir of his *karma*s that have fructified. But, when the individual ceases to exist as a result of the knowledge of *ātman*, there is no nucleus to come back to as another life form. Thus the liberation is aptly described as *apunarāvṛtti* (not returning as a limited individual). That is the highest goal of human endeavour reached by gaining the knowledge, *tat-tvam-asi*.

Fourth Verse

We have seen in the earlier verse that the entire universe of plurality is shining in and after the *ātman*, which is *Brahman.* There is a general misconception that the sentient being obtaining in the body is essentially a limited being, called *jīva.* Śrī Śaṅkara addresses this issue in the fourth verse and establishes that the sentience of the *jīva* is the only reality about *jīva.*

नानाच्छिद्रघटोदरस्थितमहादीपप्रभाभास्वरं
ज्ञानं यस्य तु चक्षुरादिकरणद्वारा बहिः स्पंदते ।
जानामीति तमेव भांतमनुभात्येतत्समस्तं जगत्
तस्मै श्रीगुरुमूर्तये नम इदं श्रीदक्षिणामूर्तये ।। ४।।

nānācchidraghaṭodarasthitamahādīpaprabhābhāsvaraṁ
jñānaṁ yasya tu cakṣurādikaraṇadvārā bahiḥ spandate ।
jānāmīti tameva bhāntamanubhātyetatsamastaṁ jagat
tasmai śrīgurumūrtaye nama idaṁ śrīdakṣiṇāmūrtaye ॥ 4 ॥

यस्य (*yasya*) — of whom, नानाच्छिद्रघटोदरस्थितमहादीपप्रभाभास्वरं (*nānācchidraghaṭodarasthitamahādīpaprabhābhāsvaraṁ*) — brilliantly shining like the illumination of a big lamp placed inside a pot with many holes around it, ज्ञानं तु (*jñānaṁ tu*) — knowledge alone, चक्षुरादिकरणद्वारा

(*cakṣurādi-skaraṇadvārā*) — through the sense-organs like eyes, etc., बहिः (*bahiḥ*) — outside, स्पंदते (*spandate*) — goes, जानामी (*jānāmi*) — I know, इति (*iti*) — thus, भांतम् (*bhāntam*) — shining, तमेव (*tameva*) — that alone, एतत (*etat*) — this, समस्तम् *samastam* — entire, जगत् (*jagat*) — universe, अनुभति (*anubhāti*) — shining after, तस्मै श्रीगुरुमूर्तये नम इदं श्रीदक्षिणामूर्तये (*tasmai śrīgurumūrtaye nama idaṁ śrīdakṣiṇāmūrtaye*).

When a brilliant lamp is placed inside an inverted pot having many holes, the light pours out through those holes. In the same way, the awareness of *Brahman* is spilling out in the individual through the sense-organs like eyes. That awareness, *Brahman*, is the witness of all this world of things that shines after the *ātman*.

There is a set of sentences in the Upaniṣads, called the *praveśa śrutis*, meaning those sentences which talk of *Brahman* entering into the bodies of living beings after creating them.

तत्सृष्ट्वा । तदेवानुप्राविशत् । — *तैत्तिरीयोपनिषद्*, २-६
स एष इह प्रविष्टः । — *बृहदारण्यकोपनिषद्*, १-४-७
जीवेनात्मनानुप्रविश्य नामरूपे व्याकरवाणि । — *छांदोग्योपनिषद्*, ६-३-२

tatsṛṣṭvā, tadevānuprāviśat । — *Taittirīyopaniṣad,* 2-6
sa eṣa iha praviṣṭaḥ । — *Bṛhadāraṇyakopaniṣad,* 1-4-7
jīvenātmanānupraviṣya nāmarūpe vyākaravāṇi ।
— *Chāndogyopaniṣad,* 6-3-2

The *Para Brahman* created it and then indeed entered into it.

That this *Para Brahman* has entered into this body.

Let me enter in the form of *jīva* and manifest as name and form.

There is a room. A person enters into it. How many things are there now? Two; the person and the room. Here is the body. Bhagavān has entered into it. How many things are there? *Kṣetra*, the body and the *kṣetrajña*, the knower of the body, who is the same *Brahman*. What about me and mine? We have seen in the first verse that the notions 'me' and 'mine' have their origin in ignorance. If we keep a brilliant light covered by a pot with many holes, that light pours out through the holes and illuminates whatever object comes in its way. Similarly, here is a body, quite often compared to the pot and the Supreme Reality, the Light of lights, the *ātmajyoti* (*parañjyoti*) that is shining in the body, and illuminating various objects of the world through different sense-organs. The individual 'me' and 'mine' is an invention of the ignorant mind. Thus the individual consists of a body, the *ātman*, the mind and ignorance, all illuminated by the self-evident *ātman*.

Normally, we are conscious of the particular, namely *nāma* and *rūpa*, and fail to recognise the reality which is always present, as it were, in the background. The manifest can never be the ultimate Truth. Particular or manifest is relative to the time-space framework. A young man is looking at the mirror. He notices the image and everything about the mirror, but misses the seer. Without the seer, there is no mirror; there is no frame; and there is no image in the mirror. The seen does not exist independent of the seer.

Suppose I say *oṁ*, *oṁ*, *oṁ*, thrice. You have heard *oṁ* thrice. But you missed the silence in between two successive *oṁ*'s. This is like missing the *draṣṭā*, while looking into the mirror. You cannot hear *oṁ* unless there is silence as the background. You could not have heard that *oṁ* in a noisy market place. In that silence as the background I can say *oṁ*; I can say 'Śrī Rāma'; or I can say 'Śrī Kṛṣṇa'. Is there a difference between the silence before *oṁ* and the silence after *oṁ*? No. That silence is the background or matrix on which '*oṁ*' could be heard. The sound *oṁ* comes and goes but the silence stays. We always notice the sounds, but we don't have the composure of mind to notice the silence on which the sounds occur. Mind should not be hyperactive. 'Don't run after the running mind' says Bhagavān Ramaṇa Maharṣi.

Consider two thoughts in succession. There is a gap between the two thoughts. That gap, that silence between the thoughts, is not just silence; it is not a void. Observe the silence of the mind, the silence when the mind is not active. Between two thoughts, there is silence. In that silence, there is no time and there is no space; because time and space are the creation of the mind. There is also no causation between two thoughts. It is the matrix of awareness (*caitanya*), in which there is no space, no time, and no causation. But it is this *nirviśeṣa* (attributeless, unmanifest) *caitanya* that illumines the time, space, and causation and everything that comes in the wake of time, space, and causation.

What is the matrix of the ornament called necklace? Gold. What is the matrix of the shirt? Cloth. What is the matrix of the hero or the villain on a movie screen? Light. Suppose I see (know) a pot. What is the matrix of that pot-knowledge? Knowledge, Awareness, *caitanya*. That attributeless *caitanya* (matrix) is shining between any two successive thoughts. The *caitanya* which is in and through every thought and also in between the two thoughts is *ananta*, timeless, meaning that it is beyond the illusion of time. *Ananta* does not mean endless stretching in the time-scale. *Ananta* means beyond the illusion of time. *Ātmajyoti* is the background, the matrix and the reality of every piece of knowledge. When I feel the heat, it is the awareness, which is *ātman*, expressing through the sense of touch. The same *ātma caitanya* is spilling out of the eyes illuminating forms and colours; through ears making sounds evident. *Kenopaniṣad* describes *ātman* as the eye of the eye, ear of the ear, etc.

We may mistake that the sensation of heat and cold is the characteristic of the skin or the sensation of sound is the characteristic of the ear. No. It is like a tap giving water or window giving sunlight. The sense-organs are like windows through which the *ātma caitanya* is spilling out. You are not the person that you imagine yourself to be. You are that attributeless awareness in the wake of which the person, the intellect, the mind, the sense-organs and all the way down, the objects of the world are shining. The moment you get up from the sleep, the very first manifestation of this awareness is 'I am'. Then comes the notion 'I am the body in the world'. 'I am' is the boundary between the reality, the *ātman*, and the falsehood. You are not the body. You should steadfastly refuse to identify with the body. You behave and act in a way that you are different from the body. You should look at the body as the witness and treat the body as an instrument for a higher purpose. You are not the body. You are the *ātma jyoti*, which is the timeless, spaceless and attributeless knowledge. That *jñāna* is *Brahman. Satyaṁ jñānanamanantaṁ brahma.*

Our minds are accustomed to see the plurality of objects. Also, mind has the tendency of dividing everything into parts. Mind depends on the sense-organs for its information. The sense-organs have a limited range of perception and accordingly they show everything in parts. We should not go by what the mind tells, without inquiry and investigation. What the mind knows is either false, or at best, it is purely a relative knowledge. What all the mind knows is within the framework of time and space. A particular thing is *sāvayava*, meaning 'having parts'. Water is one of the five great elements (*mahābhūta*), but it is *sāvayava*. The water in the pot is a part of the *mahābhūta* water. The mind has the habit of extrapolating this situation to the partless, *nirvayava,* also. For example, space is all-pervading and partless. But the mind looks at space as pot-space, etc., as though space is divided into parts like water. But water happens to be *sāvayava*, while space is *niravayava*. It is not that a small piece of space is put in the pot, just as we go to a pond and collect a small amount of water from the pond. Space is there within and without every object. We superimpose the smallness or bigness of the limiting adjunct, the *upādhi* onto the space and talk in terms of small or big space. Neither bigness nor smallness belongs to *ākāśa* (space). They belong to the *upādhi* through which *ākāśa* is expressed.

This is the situation with respect to *ākāśa*. Take the case of *prakāśa,* the light. A small bulb, a big bulb, moon, sun, etc., are all different media (*maṇḍala*s) through which the light is pouring out. The *maṇḍala* can be small or big. We superimpose this limitation of the *maṇḍala* onto the light itself. In fact we are prisoners in a cell with three walls. The walls are space, time, and principle of causation. These three together constitute what is called *Māyā*.

In the same way, the individual 'I' is put in place by the mind. There is the body, mind, the Supreme Reality — that *mahādīpa* or *ātma-jyoti* (*parañ-jyoti*), and ignorance. Mind in combination with ignorance becomes the person. The person is false. We should recognise that the person is not the subject but an object. When the seer (*dṛk*) gets entangled with the seen (*dṛśya*), due to ignorance, there arises the person. On the infinite *caitanya,* the individuality, viz., *jīvatva,* is superimposed. When the person is falsified, there remains the non-dual *ātma-jyoti*. You have to accept that there is *nirviśeṣa jñāna* (attributeless awareness) within you as your essential nature because of which, all names and forms are getting illuminated. But the assumption that the awareness is confined to a given body and mind is false. When you look at a glowing ember, you are looking at the great element fire, the *mahāgni*. Similarly when you recognise the *ātma caitanya* within yourself and get resolved into it and be with it, you remain a witness to the person all the way down to the objects of the world.

Ātma caitanya is infinite and whole even when a particular sense-organ like eye is absent in a given person. Even the blind or deaf person is essentially a conscious being, though a particular expression of that consciousness, like knowledge of forms and colours or that of sounds is missing in that person. We should be cautious and avoid imputing the properties of the *upādhi* to the underlying Reality. That *ātma caitanya* expressing through this body, is indeed *Īśvara*.

Yasya jñānam, yasya parameśvarasya jñānam. It is the ocean of awareness or consciousness that is expressed through this *upādhi.* We may not allow the false individual to come in the way. As we learn to notice the falsity of the person, the person will disappear. We have to observe the mind as a witness, in order to go beyond the mind. Take the help of the mind to stretch yourself into the Reality. The teaching as well as the learning are there because of the mind alone. With the help of the mind we go beyond the mind, because mind is none other than a motion in the infinite awareness. We should take note of the fact that no knowledge is coming from outside into the person. *Cakṣurādikaraṇadvārā bahiḥ spandate.* It is the illumination of the *ātma caitanya* which is coming out through the sense-organs.

It is pertinent to remember a *Kenopaniṣad mantra* here, which is as follows:

श्रोत्रस्य श्रोत्रं मनसो मनो यद्वाचो ह वाचं स उ प्राणस्य प्राणः ।
चक्षुषश्चक्षुः . . . (१-२)

śrotrasya śrotraṁ manaso mano yadvāco ha vācaṁ sa u prāṇasya prāṇaḥ । *cakṣuṣaścakṣuḥ* . . . (1-2)

The *ātman* is indeed the ear of the ear, mind of the mind, speaker of the speech; it is the force behind the vital forces of the body; it is the eye of the eye. . . .

Jānāmīti tameva bhāntamanubhātyetatsamastaṁ jagat. There are two important Sanskrit words which help us to realise the glory of *ātman*. They are *bhāti*, meaning 'shining', and *anubhāti*, which means 'shining after'. The pot shines; that is why we are able to see it. But, it is more appropriate to say that the pot shines after the lamp. Then, the lamp shines; but it shines after the eyes. The eyes, in their turn, shine after the mind, which shines after the intellect, which shines after the *ahaṅkāra*, which finally shines after the *ātman*. But the *ātman* itself is self-shining, and everything else shines after it. This can be summarised as:

घटः भाति । घटः दीपं अनुभाति । दीपः तु भाति ।
दीपः नेत्रं अनुभाति । नेत्रं तु भाति ।
नेत्रं मनः अनुभाति । मनः तु भाति ।
मनः बुद्धिं अनुभाति । बुद्धिः तु भाति ।
बुद्धिः आत्मानं अनुभाति । आत्मा भाति ।।

ghaṭaḥ bhāti । *ghaṭaḥ dīpam anubhāti* । *dīpaḥ tu bhāti* ।
dīpaḥ netraṁ anubhāti । *netraṁ tu bhāti* ।
netraṁ manaḥ anubhāti । *manaḥ tu bhāti* ।
manaḥ buddhiṁ anubhāti । *buddhiḥ tu bhāti* ।
buddhiḥ ātmānaṁ anubhāti । *ātmā bhāti* ।

'I am' divested of all false superimpositions is the only thing that shines on its own. And that 'I am' is the reflection of the

Supreme Reality in the mind-stuff; it is the point from where you take off to the Reality, where there is no 'I'. Truth is not the reward of an effort; it is not the end of a journey. Truth is you. The only reward for Truth is Truth itself; it eliminates the bondage of ignorance.

One should identify oneself with that consciousness, not with the body. The purpose of the teaching is to make you see the truth. Abide in that awareness. You are always conscious of something or other. Don't take the consciousness for granted. Be aware of that consciousness. Due to the tyranny of the individuality, which is the result of identification with the fundamentally insentient body, we lose sight of our own nature. We are constantly busy with petty pleasures and pains, likes and dislikes so much so that we ignore the only reality, namely the awareness that makes all these possible.

That awareness is not removed or separated from you. In every moment of your life, you are a conscious being. *Sattā*, Being, is not separated from you. In fact, both awareness and Being culminate in you. Being alert towards that awareness and constantly abiding in it is the real *samādhi*. We may not bother about other varieties of *samādhi*. This is the only important *samādhi*. The reward for it is itself.

Fifth Verse

THE question that engaged the human mind from times immemorial is: What is *ātman*? *Ātman* is that which is most intrinsic to you, innermost to you and is nearest to you; it is, indeed, you. Nobody can deny his own existence (*na aham asmi*). Nobody can say: 'I don't know myself', since *ātman* is self-evident. Of course, somebody may say: 'I don't want to be'. Now, what is my essential nature? People claim that they know themselves. But the fact appears to be that mostly people are ignorant about themselves. There are any number of people who visit a psychologist. The psychologist helps you to know about yourself better than what you already know. He helps you to come to terms with yourself.

If somebody claims that he knows himself, he is mistaken. When someone says that he is walking, he is identifying himself with his legs, which is one of the *karmendriya*s, the organs of action. When you say that I am seeing, the meaning of 'I' has changed; now you have identified yourself with eyes, which is one of the *jñānendriya*s, sense-organs. When you say you are comfortable, you are identifying yourself with the mind. You have now shifted your centre of 'I' from sense-organs to the mind. Suppose somebody says that he is a doctor or a professor, he has shifted the centre of 'I' from the mind to the intellect. Thus there is no clear-cut meaning for the word 'I', as understood by people. This unique confusion about oneself is universal.

In Vedānta we don't deal with topical, situational, or

incidental errors. We deal with universal errors. An error uniformly committed throughout the world by every human being is addressed in Vedānta. It deals with what is most intrinsic to human beings. What do I lose, if I don't know *ātman*? If you don't know *ātman*, the purpose of human life itself is defeated. We know that the horoscope changes from person to person. But, there is one thing common to every horoscope of every person that has ever taken birth. That is, he is destined to know his own *svarūpa*. There is no exception to this. What all you have to do is to work in favour of your destiny, to manifest your destiny. If you put so many obstacles against destiny, the destiny may be defeated. Given a chance, that destiny is waiting to manifest. You should make this destiny, to know what *ātman* is, a reality. If you have not known many things of the world, you have not lost much. But if you have not known *ātman*, you have lost everything. So it is important that one should know what *ātman* is. Not knowing *ātman* in one's life is like keeping the horse and losing the rider; it is like keeping the shadow and losing the person. One who has known *ātman* in his lifetime can say at the end of the life that he lived well. Śrī Śaṅkara dedicated one verse in this small text to analyse various contentions about the essential nature of *ātman*.

देहं प्राणमपींद्रियाण्यपि चलां बुद्धिं च शून्यं विदुः
स्त्रीबालांधजडोपमास्त्वहमिति भ्रांता भृशं वादिनः ।
मायाशक्तिविलासकल्पितमहाव्यामोहसंहारिणे
तस्मै श्रीगुरुमूर्तये नम इदं श्रीदक्षिणामूर्तये ।। ५ ।।

dehaṁ prāṇamapīndriyāṇyapi calāṁ buddhiṁ ca śūnyaṁ viduḥ
strībālāndhajaḍopamāstvahamiti bhrāntā bhr̥śaṁ vādinaḥ ।

māyāśaktivilāsakalpitamahāvyāmohasaṁhāriṇe
tasmai śrīgurumūrtaye nama idaṁ śrīdakṣiṇā-
mūrtaye ॥ 5 ॥

भ्रांता (*bhrāntā*) — the deluded, भृशं वादिनः (*bhṛśaṁ vādinaḥ*) — vehemently arguing, अहं इति (*aham iti*) — that the आत्मन् (*ātman*) is, देहं (*dehaṁ*) — body, प्राणम् (*prāṇam*) — the vital force, अपि (*api*) — and, इंद्रियाणि (*indriyāṇi*) — the sense-organs, अपि (*api*) — also, चलां बुद्धिं (*calāṁ buddhiṁ*) — the mind in flux, च (*ca*) — and, शून्यं (*śūnyaṁ*) — void, विदुः (*viduḥ*) — take it, स्त्रीबालांधजडोपमः (*strībālāndha-jaḍopamaḥ*) — like even the uneducated women, children, and dull people, मायाशक्तिविलासकल्पितमहाव्यामोहसंहारिणे (*māyāśaktivilāsakalpita-mahāvyāmohasaṁhāriṇe*) — the one who destroys the great delusion caused by the play of the power of *māyā*, तस्मै श्रीगुरुमूर्तये नम इदं श्रीदक्षिणामूर्तये (*tasmai śrīgurumūrtaye nama idaṁ śrīdakṣiṇāmūrtaye*).

They vehemently argue that the body, the vital force, the organs of action and the sense-organs, the pulse-like mind and even the void are the meaning of 'I'. They are all mistaken like the uneducated women, children, the blind and the dull persons. Lord Dakṣiṇāmūrti, who is the Universal teacher and also the *ātman* of every being, destroys the delusion caused by the play of the power of *Māyā*. My prostrations unto that Lord.

Śaṅkara lived a couple of hundred years before Jesus, the Christ. At that time itself, the Indian society was very advanced in many fields like mathematics, astronomy, etc., what to speak of spirituality or philosophy? Very important philosophical schools of thought were already established by that time. Cārvāka was the earliest atheist in the history of humanity. The Hindu society did not ban his works; on the other hand, the society revered him as a sage because of the good values cherished by him, though it rejected his ideas. He argued that the *ātman* is body itself. For the glutton, stomach is the *ātman*. His logic is given in the *Sarvadarśanasaṁgraha* of Mādhavācārya as follows:

> अहं स्थूलः कृशोऽस्मीति सामानाधिकरण्यतः ।
> देहः स्थौल्यादियोगाच्च स एवात्मा न चापरः ।। — चार्वाकदर्शनम्
>
> *ahaṁ sthūlaḥ kr̥śo'smīti sāmānādhikaraṇyataḥ* ।
> *dehaḥ sthaulyādiyogācca sa evātmā na cāparaḥ* ।।
> — *Cārvākadarśanam*
>
> 'I am heavy; I am lean': this is how people say. In these usages, the words 'I' and 'heavy' are referring to the same object. The heaviness etc. are, after all, associated with the body only. Therefore, the physical body is indeed the *ātman*. There is no other *ātman*.

When we say the body is *ātman*, there is no body in sleep. What is lying on the bed in sleep is not the body; it is an assembly of five elements. It becomes a body only when you come to think of it as a body. *Deha* is not different from *dehābhimāna*, the mistaken notion of 'me' and 'mine'. Therefore, the body has its existence in mind, which in turn, exists in consciousness.

Some people looked at the issue a little more deeply and concluded that the vital force is the *ātman*, since it is what makes the body a living entity. In this school of thought, the aspect of action that is performed by the limbs of the body is highlighted. This view is not tenable. When a man is famished, the strength of life force may come down but his sense of 'I' will not come down. It may even express more forcefully, yearning for food.

There are a few other people who look at the body as a source of enjoyment. They opine that the sense-organs, through which a living being enjoys a few things of the world, constitute the *ātman*. These schools of thought are also untenable. The physical body cannot be the *ātman*, since it is an insentient pot-like object known to me, while I am the knower, essentially distinct from the known. The organs of action and the sense-organs cannot be the *ātman*, since nobody looks upon himself as plural. Also, the handicapped people have *ātman* the same way as common people.

Then, we have the *kṣaṇika vijñānavādin*s, who maintain that the mind which is in constant flux is the *ātman*. They come close to Vedānta in some respects. Nāgārjuna was one of the leading lights of this school. These are the people who first suggested the concept of frequency, much before it became well known in physics. For example, when I move my hand, it looks as though it is one event. But it is a series of events. The entire movement can be subdivided into hundreds or thousands of movements. Every movement is recorded by the mind as a thought frame. The movement of the hand as understood by the mind is a quick succession of thousands of such thought frames that formed in the mind. When they occur in quick succession, we get a feeling of continuity, though there is no such continuity. Suppose you drop a fistful of pebbles. Is the flow of pebbles continuous or discontinuous? It is discontinuous. Suppose I drop sand from the hand? The flow of sand looks continuous, but in reality, it is discontinuous. There is always a small gap, both in terms of space and time, between any two sand particles. Suppose I pour a glass of water. The water flow looks continuous, but it is discontinuous because the molecules of water fall one after another. The entire motion, though registered as one continuous event, is in fact a quick succession of thousands of motions. The figures and movements that we see on the movie screen look continuous. But in reality, the frames of the film are projected onto the screen one after another, and at any given moment, there is just one frame on the screen. But the quick succession (frequency) of the frames makes it look continuous. Mind also works on the same principle. It is the glory of the Buddhists that they understood this aspect of the functioning of the mind very correctly. They are the first thinkers to come out with the idea of frequency-related continuity versus real discontinuity.

In fact, there is nothing like a single entity called mind. Mind is nothing but a series of thoughts. Each thought is distinct from every other thought. The process of thinking is exactly similar to that of a picture on a movie screen. This is what is called *calāṁ buddhiṁ ca*. That *buddhi* is a flicker in the consciousness. Even the light of an electric bulb is discontinuous. The light goes on and off fifty times per second. But it looks as though it is continuously glowing. Mind is also like that bulb. The *vijñāna-vādin*s maintain that there is no *ātman* other than this bleep-bleep flickering of the thoughts.

There is another school of thought among Buddhists. They are called *śūnyavādin*s. Their contention is that void is the reality of everything and void alone is the *ātman*. This contention is not acceptable. Is the void known or not? If it is known, then how is it known? Does it reflect light? If so, there are photon particles in it and therefore, it cannot be a void any longer. If it does not reflect light, then it could not have been known at all. Also, if it is known, then the knower is present and therefore, void is no more relevant. If the knower is absent, then how does the void get validated? *Śūnya* cannot be the Reality.

Bhṛśaṁ vādinaḥ. Everyone of these thinkers is an erudite scholar. They put forward cogent-sounding arguments in support of their contentions. But, unfortuantely they are totally ignorant of *ātman*. However scholarly they may be, they are grievously mistaken about the true nature of *ātman*.

Strībālāndhajaḍopamāḥ. These words *strī*, *bāla*, *andha* and *jaḍa* are not aimed to denigrate certain sections of the society. Each of these words symbolises a particular contention or theory. *Strī* stands for a woman of fashion spending most of the time before a mirror taking care of the body using many cosmetics. She has a notion of beauty. She is convinced that the subjecive quality of the body, called beauty, is her essential reality; that is, the beauty of the skin is, as it were, *ātman* for her. In the fashion industry circles, the body is worshipped as *ātman*. Her entire commitment is to look good. She represents the *dehātma-vāda*, the contention that body alone is the *ātman*. Here, Śrī Śaṅkara is not pointing the finger at the gender of a person. In the Upaniṣadic literature, we come across quite a few wise women like Maitreyī as in *Bṛhadāraṇyaka Upaniṣad*.

Bāla means a child. A child is mostly engaged in eating and drinking, taking care of hunger and thirst. Therefore *bāla* stands for *prāṇa-ātma-vāda*, the contention that the vital force is the *ātman*. *Andha*, a blind person, stands for the contention that the sense-organs are the *ātman*. Suppose I am near-sighted. I cannot see objects at a distance clearly. Am I the witness of the change in the eyesight or am I the eyesight itself? Any change is recognised as change if only there is a changeless witness in the background. The change in eyesight has taken place *vis-a-vis* the underlying reality of the sense of 'I' and is recognised as such by the same reality. Any change takes place against a changeless background alone. This fact is not recognised by these thinkers and the sense-organs are assumed to be the *ātman*. When a person loses his eyesight, does he cease to exist? No. He was there before, and now also he continues to exist albeit without eyesight. Suppose a person lost one eye. He may feel quite miserable about it. But he does not feel that he lost half of himself, remaining only as a half (truncated) 'I'.

Jaḍa means a dullard. It points to *vijñānavādin*. He lost the faculty of thinking and failed to see the Truth; hence he is *jaḍa*. He identifies *ātman* with the mind which is a product of the insentient *prakṛti*. Hence he is *jaḍa*. It is well known in the Vedāntic literature that the mind is made up of the *sāttvika* parts of the five great elements.

All these people err in understanding *ātman*, because they are trying to define and formulate *ātman*. Any such attempt is bound to lead to wrong conclusions, because *ātman* is beyond the ken of the mind. We are prisoners of the mind. We live in a prison made up of three walls, viz., space, time and causation. The mind tries to analyse everything with respect to the time-space-causation framework. The *ātman*, which illuminates this framework and which is the witness of this framework and continues to shine even after the framework is resolved, cannot be understood or characterised by the mind. The mind should be made ready to resolve itself; then only you will be able to abide as *ātman*. The mind throws a veil of *Māyā,* so much so, the truth of *ātman* is hidden from us. We look at the world and at ourselves through the net of our desires, fears and notions. Through that net, we get a distorted picture of both the world and the *ātman*. If somebody claims that he has known *ātman*, please understand that he has not known *ātman* (*avijñātaṁ vijānatām*; *Kena Upaniṣad*).

If somebody claims that God is in heaven, he knows him

as an unknown entity. What kind of knowing is it? This is preaching and not teaching. If some other person says that God is unknown to him, he means that God is sitting somewhere permanently away from him and he has no way of coming across him. But, God cannot be characterised as known or unknown. In fact, there is only one God. That God is before you in the form of universe or God is within you as *ātman*. If you want to see God, see God as the substratum of this universe. Or, you realise your essential nature and be God, the *ātman*. There is no other way of knowing God in one's life.

Ātman happens to be most intrinsic to the person. But the person is ignorant of *ātman*. Why is this paradox? One is searching for *ātman* away from oneself. In such a situation, you will never be able to recognise *ātman*. Anything that can be described, as this or that, cannot be *ātman*. After all you cannot be something else. You can only be a seer of something else. It is ridiculous to say that something else is I. People, who characterise *prāṇa* or *buddhi* and then say that it is *ātman*, have missed *ātman*. There is a single source, namely the *ātman*, from which this *prāṇa* and *buddhi* originate. If you look at the *prāṇa* you can reach that source of *prāṇa*. If you look at the mind, the *buddhi*, you can reach the source of that *buddhi*.

Ātman is the *cit* or *caitanya*, which is beyond all distortions and all attributes that are superimposed on it by ignorance. For example, when I am seeing, I am conscious of the forms of the objects. That is what seeing means. Everybody is a conscious being. But, we make the mistake of identifying ourselves with the *indriya*s. I am a conscious being; so, when that consciousness expresses through the eye, it appears to acquire the properties of the eye. When it expresses through the ears, it becomes as though one with the ears. But, if the eyes develop the problem of short sight, I conclude that I have short sight. This is the *vyāmoha*, delusion. We attribute the properties of the limiting adjuncts, e.g., the *indriyas* to the *cit*. We are conscious beings; but are we aware of that truth? Be aware that you are conscious of sound. Be aware of the fact that you are conscious of forms. Be aware of all the sensations without identifying yourself with the sensations. When you rise from the level of 'being conscious of' to the level of 'being awareful of being conscious of forms etc.', you slowly rise above the attributes of the limiting adjuncts. The *ātman*, which is *sat-cit*, does not differ from person to person.

All this world is the product of *Māyā*. At the level of an individual, it appears as the delusion of mixing up the seen with the seer, the pure 'I am'. Anything you add to 'I am' is wrong. The only truth about yourself is 'I am'. There is no other truth. So I am what I am. Be aware of 'I am' and remain in 'I am'. Be sure that 'I am' will resolve into *ātma caitanya*. Knowing *ātman* is identical with rejecting *anātman*. There is no knowing of *ātman* other than rejecting *anātman*, because *ātman* happens to be your *svarūpa*. So the path to reach *ātman* is totally of rejection and negation. Reject ruthlessly all that is *anātman* and stop all your efforts to know *ātman*. As long as you make efforts to know *ātman*, you will never know it. This is the process that is to be followed. You need a serene mind for this *sādhanā*. You need the grace of *Īśvara* to overcome the thralldom of *Māyā*. Some people say that *Māyā* is an invention of Śrī Śaṅkara. They dub Śrī Śaṅkara as *māyāvādin*. But, Śrī Śaṅkara is *brahmavādin*. *Māyā* is not a theory based on speculation. *Māyā* is a statement of fact.

Ātman is most intrinsic to you. But you are ignorant of it. Is death real or life real? When you are hale and healthy, life appears to be the real thing. But an occasion comes when death appears to be real and life unreal. That is *Māyā*. The concepts of time and space are *Māyā*. We talk of past, present, and future. Where is the past? When you say something happened last year, you are talking of that past as understood in the present. In the mind there is some information which is characterised as memory. Mind is like a cabinet with different partitions. All objects in different partitions are essentially present in the same cabinet. In the same way, due to memory, certain notions appear to be from the past, while in reality they are in the present. The mind tries to stretch out itself to the future. When the mind is anticipating in the present, that anticipation is labelled as future. The predictions of the future may never turn out to be true. All these anticipations and the expectations of the future are present now in the mind. Suppose you don't have a memory. Will you have a past? No. Suppose you don't have anticipation or expectation. Will you have a future? No. Then where is the past and future? The past and future are not outside but they appear to be so. That is *Māyā*.

Time appears to be outside. Is it in the clock? In the small needle or in the big needle? Is it in the dial? No, it is in the motion. Motion is a notion. Motion does not have the property called time. The mind records the motion of the needle. The interval, in terms of memory, between different positions of the needle is time. So the time is within you, the past is within you, the future is within you, and the present is within you. The world you see outside is within you. We make a big deal about 'inside' and 'outside'. What is the boundary between the two? The body. What kind of boundary is it? You wrongly identify yourself with the body and define 'inside' and 'outside' accordingly. The 'inside' and 'outside' is purely a product of ignorance, *avidyā*.

Where is the future? Now. Where is the past? Now. Therefore, the present is defined in terms of past and future. Where is the present? Now. What is this 'now'? It must be the briefest possible moment. What is such a moment? It is the awareful being, which is *sat-cit ātman*. The division of indivisible *ātman* into three periods on a time-scale is *Māyā*. Time, space, and causation are *Māyā*. Your mind is the cause of your *vyāmoha*, delusion. The mind is in between the body and you, the *ātman* which is *Para Brahman*. The mind is nothing but *Māyā*. The power of *Māyā* is infinite. It can be dispelled by the grace of the Lord alone. *Māyāśaktivilāsa-kalpitamahāvyāmohasaṁhāriṇe.*

Any amount of exposition may leave you still wanting with regard to that knowledge. In the acquisition of that knowledge the teacher will help you from outside. The outside *guru* can only show the way. Get hold of that inner *guru*. That inner *guru* is *ātman* and that is Dakṣiṇāmūrti. Then grace descends upon you. The grace of the *guru* works wonders. It pulls you up into the Supreme Reality. That way alone you will be saved.

There is one particular *buddhi vṛtti*, called *akhaṇḍa ākāra vṛtti*. We have a series of thoughts based on subject-object division (*khaṇḍita buddhi vṛtti*s), one after the other endlessly. They are the mind's creation and the whole life is filled with them. Go on rejecting the falsehood of *khaṇḍita buddhi vṛtti*s in accordance with the teaching. Then the *akhaṇḍa ākāra budhhi vṛtti*, that knowledge in which the subject-object division is absent, will be given to you by *Īśvara*. Then, the smaller 'I', the individual, gets resolved in the infinite awareness.

Stop making effort to know *ātman*. The effort, *sādhana*, works up to a point in rejecting the falsehood. The human mind never stops making effort. It continues to define, formulate, verbalise and reach out. The realisation that you should stop this effort is itself a grace. People make all kinds of mistakes in understanding *ātman* simply because of the absence of grace.

Ātma caitanya illuminates each and everything that comes in its way. The body is, as it were, possessed by *ātma caitanya*. The awareness is spilling out from every pore of the body. Even the tip of the toe-nail has consciousness. If a mosquito sits anywhere on my body, I can immediately recognise it. If there is a small change in the temperature of the surroundings, I can recognise it. Nobody takes a pot to be *ātman*. Suppose my finger is severed from the hand and is lying on the table. I don't have the sense of the 'I' associated with the finger lying on the table. Suppose the finger is restored to the body by surgery, then I associate the sense of 'I' with the finger. So wherever *ātma caitanya* is expressed, one mistook that to be *ātman*. Because the body is thus possessed by consciousness, everybody mistakes the body to be *ātman*, while a few philosophised the mistake into a school of thought.

Prāṇa, the life force which is working wonders in the body, in terms of inhalation and exhalation of the respiratory system, working of the digestive system, etc., originates from *ātman*. As the *ātma caitanya* is manifesting as *prāṇa-śakti,* some people misunderstood *prāṇa* as *ātman*. As the *ātman*, the awareness is expressing through various limbs of the body, we take them to be *ātman*.

When the mind is not covered by *tamas*, or when it is not scattered all over by *rajas* (*vikṣepa*), and when it is in harmony associated with *sattva*, it captures the greatest of the truths of this universe. This is made possible by the reflection of *ātma caitanya* in *buddhi*. So some people mistake the mind itself for *ātman*. Thus, at every stage the expressions of *ātman* are mistaken to be the *ātman* itself. These are the varieties in the expression of the *ātma caitanya* through the limiting adjuncts. They are not *ātman*.

Me and mine are absolutely false notions. We have committed ourselves to this smallness. We are afraid of the big. We are afraid of the truth. As long as we are afraid, the truth will be away from us. We pray to the Lord Dakṣiṇāmūrti to remove the false identification with the body, *prāṇa, indriya*s, *manas, buddhi,* and the person. The person is supposed to be the subject. It is supposed to be me. Recognise that the person is an object and is external to you and reach the goal of *ātma sākṣātkāra*.

Sixth Verse

THE *śūnyavādin* relies heavily upon the sleep state to substantiate his contention that void is the reality. In order to refute the *śūnyavāda*, Śrī Śaṅkara devotes one verse to the all-important analysis of sleep. In Vedānta, the analysis of sleep *vis-a-vis* the other two states of experience, namely waking and dream states, (*avasthā traya viveka*) plays a pivotal role in understanding the true nature of *ātman*.

राहुग्रस्तदिवाकरेंदुसदृशो मायासमाच्छादनात्
सन्मात्रः करणोपसंहरणतो योऽभूत्सुषुप्तः पुमान् ।
प्रागस्वाप्समिति प्रबोधसमये यः प्रत्यभिज्ञायते
तस्मै श्रीगुरुमूर्तये नम इदं श्रीदक्षिणामूर्तये ।। ६ ।।

rāhugrastadivākarendusadṛśo māyāsamācchādanāt
sanmātraḥ karaṇopasaṁharaṇato yo'bhūtsuṣuptaḥ pumān ।
prāgasvāpsamiti prabodhasamaye yaḥ pratyabhi jñāyate
tasmai śrīgurumūrtaye nama idaṁ śrīdakṣiṇā-mūrtaye ॥ 6 ॥

यः पुमान् (*yaḥ pumān*) — whosoever person, सुषुप्तः (*suṣuptaḥ*) — having slept, राहुग्रस्तदिवाकरेंदुसदृशः (*rāhugrastadivākaren-dusadṛśaḥ*) — like even the sun and moon eclipsed by Rāhu, मायासमाच्छादनात् (*māyāsamācchādanāt*) — on account of the covering up by *māyā*, करणोपसंहरणतः (*karaṇopa-saṁharaṇataḥ*) — because of the withdrawal of the sense-organs and the mind, सन्मात्रः (*sanmātraḥ*) — Existence Absolute alone, अभूत् (*abhūt*) — became, यः (*yaḥ*) — who, प्रबोधसमये (*prabodhasamaye*) — at the time of waking up, प्राक् (*prāk*) — earlier, अस्वाप्सम् (*asvāpsam*) — I slept, इति (*iti*) — thus, प्रत्यभिज्ञायते (*pratyabhijñāyate*) — recollects, तस्मै श्रीगुरुमूर्तये नम इदं श्रीदक्षिणामूर्तये (*tasmai śrīgurumūrtaye nama idaṁ śrīdakṣiṇāmūrtaye*).

The *ātman*, which is the Existence Absolute, is covered by the *Māyā*, like even the Sun or the Moon is covered by the Rāhu during the eclipse. This *Puruṣa* has withdrawn all the senses and went into deep sleep. He wakes up again and remembers : I slept all this while. This *Puruṣa* is indeed the same as Lord Dakṣiṇāmūrti who has taken the incarnation of the Teacher. My salutations unto that Lord.

Human being puts all his investment in one state of experience alone, namely, waking state, *jāgrat avasthā*. He takes it for granted that whatever is experienced in *jāgrat avasthā* alone is true. We have a dream state, but we never bother to investigate it properly. In fact, *Īśvara* created the dream to teach us a profound truth. Same is the case with the sleep state. In our opinion sleep is there only to reinforce *jāgrat avasthā*. In the morning you have to go to office and work till evening; so you have to sleep in the night. A businessman has to open his shop in the morning; so, he has to sleep in the night. A person who is engaged in sensuous pleasures also should sleep, so that he can continue to enjoy next day with reinforced vigour. This is all we know or care to know about sleep. This is a big mistake. If we take into account that a child sleeps almost the entire day, sleep occupies almost same time in our life as waking state.

Therefore, any conclusions that we may reach about the reality or purpose of life by disregarding the sleep state are bound to be wrong. So it is necessary to understand this sleep. Bhagavān has created sleep as a model for us to understand our own *svarūpa*.

An example is given: *rāhugrastadivākarendu-sadṛśaḥ*. When the light between a luminous body like the Sun and the eye of the observer is intercepted, or that between an illuminating body like the Sun and the illumined body, the moon, is intercepted, we get an eclipse. These eclipses of the Sun and the moon are routinely predicted in Indian almanacs. When it comes to fixing the duration of a *tithi* (a day in lunar cycle), these almanacs do not see eye to eye. Thus they become a source of controversy in the society. Whether to celebrate *Vināyaka Caturthī* or *Śrī Rāma Navamī* on a given day or the next day? This controversy haunts us year after year. It is unfortunate that the scholars of Astrology cannot guide the society properly without creating confusion. But when it comes to predicting the eclipses, all almanacs agree. No astrologer can afford to predict an eclipse wrongly, since it can be observed and verified. The ancient astrologers Āryabhaṭa and Varāhamihira gave precise formulae to predict eclipses.

There is a popular story, attributed to our *śāstra*s, about the eclipses. A snake is supposed to swallow the Sun and the moon and then vomit it out after a little while. This story brought some bad name to our *śāstra*s. But the fact is otherwise. Description of the phenomenon of eclipse in our ancient scriptures is scientifically correct. A celestial body coming in between the observer and the luminous body casts its shadow on the latter. This shadow is called Rāhu. It is interesting to note that Indian astrology describes Rāhu as a shadow-planet (*chāyā-graha*). Śrī Śaṅkara's analogy is perfect. Like even the shadow of Rāhu covers the Sun or the moon, the veil of *Māyā* covers the true nature of *ātman*. It is important to note that *Māyā* does not cover the *ātman* entirely; it covers the *cit* (awareness) and *ānanda* (happiness or limitlessness) aspects of *ātman*. The Existence aspect of *ātman* is not covered by *Māyā* (*sanmātraḥ*). Thus, the limitless *ātman* appears to be the limited individual subject to sorrow due to the veil of *Māyā*.

In sleep there is a gap. Gap of what? Gap of the person. The person was there till he went into sleep. Devadatta went to sleep and Devadatta woke up from the sleep. There is no Devadatta during sleep. The *śūnyavādin* immediately concludes that there is nothing (*śūnya*) in sleep, and the waking state originated from that *śūnya*. But we should not forget that, in sleep, the experience of nothingness is very much present; and hence the witness of such an experience must be there. There is *ātman* fully awake in the sleep state also; *ātman* never sleeps. It illuminates everything in the waking state and the relative nothing-ness in the sleep state. Sleep is nothing but a gap in memory. Memory is one of the most important functions of the mind. A person is created out of memory. A person is what his memory is. Suppose the past of a person present in the memory is wiped out. Then, where is the person? And this person just does not exist in sleep due to a gap in memory.

The universal experience of sleep is: 'I slept happily; I did not know a thing'. Nobody experiences his complete absence in sleep. It is not possible to experience one's own non-existence, in sleep or elsewhere. Suppose you were absent in the sleep. How do you know that you were absent? You cannot say that. It is like saying that I have no knowledge. Without knowledge as the underlying reality, you cannot make that statement. In sleep there are two things: one is *ajñāna,* in the seed form; the second is happiness. In waking state, that *ajñāna* manifests as an individual in the world of plurality. How do you know that there is *ajñāna* and *sukha* in the sleep? You have experienced it. Absence of a series of specific experiences is also an experience. You cannot say that the Sun is absent during eclipse. The Sun of *ātman* shines ever. Only the windows of the sense-organs are closed (*karaṇopasaṁharaṇa*).

The darkness of a cave is a special kind of darkness. We do not come across that kind of a darkness in our day-to-day life. Even in the moonless overcast dark night, there is always some diffused light. In the cave, the intensity of light is zero. It is pitch-dark. It is as if a mountain load of pitch has fallen. We can see nothing in that darkness. But I was there in that darkness, witnessing that darkness. Going into sleep is similar to going into that cave. So *Śūnyavāda* does not stand. An eyewitness made a statement in the court to the effect that no one was present at a particular place in the middle of the night. This statement is technically wrong, since there must be at least one human being, namely, the witness himself, to be able to make that statement. Same is also the case with sleep.

During waking state you take yourself to be a *kartā*, the agent of various actions, like earning bread for the family, etc. The notions of 'me' and 'mine', and the *abhimāna* that I am doing all these things are very fundamental to the ignorant person, the *saṁsārī*. Body is me: this is *deha-abhimāna*. Body is mine is also *deha-abhimāna*. This house is mine: this is *gṛha-abhimāna*. This is my wife; this is my daughter; this is my husband. Each one of these notions is *abhimāna*. A person is nothing but a bundle of such notions. This is really the *saṁsāra*. The sleep-state invariably proves that every one of these *abhimāna*s is false. If I am essentially a *kartā*, agent, or *bhoktā*, enjoyer, then I should continue to be one in sleep also. This is not our experience. Similarly, various roles played by the person, like father or mother, brother or sister, etc., are not intrinsic to the person, since they are all absent in sleep. Thus, the sleep experience conclusively shows that the *ātman* is essentially unattached to the things of the waking state (*āsaṅgo hyayaṁ puruṣaḥ*). This truth is so emphatically presented to us by *Īśvara* day after day in the form of sleep, if only we care to investigate and understand. Analysis of sleep is an important topic in the teaching of the Upaniṣads. It is no surprise that the philosophers of the West could not fathom the depths of *ātma-jñāna*, since they have totally ignored sleep in their analysis of human experience.

Śrī Śaṅkara says that the *ātman* is the common matrix of both the waking and the sleep states. *Ātman* is like the Sun. The Sun illuminates the objects of the world, some of them known to us and some unknown. Similarly *ātman* illuminates both the known and unknown. Suppose I do not know Russian. *Ātman* illuminates the ignorance of Russian language. We should not misunderstand that *ātman,* being all knowledge, is opposed to ignorance (*tamas*). *Ātman* is not opposed to *ajñāna* (ignornace); so, *ātman* does not eliminate *ajñāna.* On the other hand, *ātman* illuminates *ajñāna* also. If *ātman* were opposed to ignorance, then none of us would be *ajñānī*s.

We know the difference between light and darkness. But a person born blind cannot distinguish between light and darkness. If *ātman* were not there in sleep, we would not be able to differentiate between waking state and sleep state. In the process of refuting *śūnyavāda*, we have understood something about the intrinsic nature of *ātman*. *Asaṅgo hyayaṁ puruṣaḥ*. This *ātman* is unattached. *Ātman* is *sanmātraḥ,* Being (Existence Absolute) alone. The Being which is *ātman* does not require proof; it proves itself and proves everything else also. Whatever is the *ātman* in sleep, that undifferentiated Existence Absolute alone is the reality. Whatever is there outside sleep is unreal, *mithyā*. The subject-object division, the plurality, *nāma-rūpa* of the world, a body identified with oneself as distinct from the world, the sense of agency and enjoyership, all these are absent in sleep. That is the truth about *ātman*. They are superimposed on *ātman* in the waking state due to ignorance.

The one irrefutable truth about me is that 'I am now and here'. The word 'now' is used with respect to past and future. Mind is like a cabinet with three compartments. They are the past, present and future. All are in the same mind which is now and here. But mind puts a stamp of 'past' on certain of its modifications, *vṛttis*. So the difference between past and present is verbal. There is no difference in the *vastu*. Past is a notion from memory in the form of a thought wave, which has its existence in *ātma caitanya* alone. Present is another thought-form. It also exists in the same ocean of consciousness. Human beings always stretch out into the future. That future is also in the present only. The difference between past, present and future is purely notional. It is not real. Present, past and future exist in one *ātman*, one unqualified attributeless monolithic 'presence', in one Being. Like even water which assumes all sorts of forms of the containers without really being affected by any form, the *ātman*, the Existence Absolute, appears as all these existent forms of 'me' and 'not-me'. Drop that 'now' and 'here'. 'I am' is the only reality. Call it *Īśvara* or *ātman*. That infinite Being is the locus or substratum of this entire universe and 'I am' is the door to it.

Generally people think that the *ātman* goes to heaven or

hell. In that case, they have not understood the *ātman* correctly. It is not the *ātman* which goes to heaven, etc. Let us take the example of wave and water. It is the wave which travels; water remains where it is, and it is everywhere (in the context of the waves). Similarly, it is only the subtle body, *sūkṣma śarīra*, which comes into this world and goes to the other world. *Ātman* which is *Brahman* is all-pervading. The only problem in understanding this truth is our false identification with the body. You need not do anything with the body. In any case, body is not yours. It is *Īśvara*'s. It is an integral part of the nature; it is an extension of the nature consisting of five great elements.

Pratyabhijñāyate. The person is associated with the body through the mind. In the absence of the mind as in sleep, there is no body-consciousness. Suppose sleep is void. Suppose *Caitra* sleeps; that is, *Caitra* is resolved into void. Next morning, why *Caitra* alone should come out of sleep? Why not *Maitra*? *Caitra* goes to sleep and *Maitra* comes out of sleep. Does it happen like that? No, because in sleep mind is there in the seed form.

The experience of sleep proves many things. You are not the body, because in sleep there is no body; yet you are there. You are not the *indriyas* (*karaṇopasaṁharaṇataḥ*). You are not *manas*; you are not the *buddhi*; you are not the *ahaṅkāra*; you are not a *saṁsārī* (*sukhī-duḥkhī*). Then, you are not *kartā*; you are not *bhoktā*. You are the pure Being. You are not even a devotee, *bhakta*. You are not a scholar of the Vedas (*yatra na vedāḥ*). You are not a father or a mother. A thief sleeps; now he is not a thief. A policeman sleeps; now he is not a policeman. Sleep is nothing but your own *svarūpa* together with the veil of *Māyā*. Sleep emphatically proves the wonderful fact: *asaṅgo hyayaṁ puruṣaḥ*. You may play any number of roles in the waking state. But, in sleep, you are blissfully detached from all those roles, since you are essentially unattached.

In *jāgrat avasthā* there is the pair of opposites, *dvandva* of *sukha* and *duḥkha*. Life is a wheel of alternating *sukha* and *duḥkha*. They are described as *āgamāpāyinaḥ*. *Sukha* comes, stays for a while, and yields its place to the opposite. Sleep proves one more point. *Sukha* is more subtle than *duḥkha*. *Sukha* is intrinsic to you, but not *duḥkha*, because you are always happy in sleep. Even an iota of pain won't touch you in sleep. Even a wretch enjoys the bliss of the sleep, as well as anybody else. The situation of the waking state, happiness or sorrow, does not alter the situation in sleep. In sleep you are invariably happy by nature. In waking state you need a reason to be happy, however silly it may be. Happiness does not require any reason. A child is happy without any reason. Happiness is intrinsic to *ātman* (*svarūpa-bhūta sukha*).

These are the points that arise out of the understanding of sleep. We may take sleep for granted, and thus ignore the lessons that it can teach, at our own peril. To the extent you can assimilate one or more of these points, to that extent, *saṁsāra,* the life of becoming, gets diluted. It is a big step in terms of understanding one's own true nature. The message of sleep can be summarised as:

1. You are by nature *asaṅga,* unattached. One has to live it out in actual life.
2. One can be happy without the fulfilment of any particular desire. This is how the *sthitaprajña* is defined.

आत्मन्येवात्मना तुष्टः स्थितप्रज्ञस्तदोच्यते ।

— *श्रीमद्भगवद्गीता,* २-५५

ātmanyevātmanā tuṣṭaḥ sthitaprajñastadocyate ।
— *Śrīmadbhagavad-Gītā*, 2-55

One who is happy in himself with himself is called *sthitaprajña*.

We desire all sorts of things. Desire is a manifestation of inadequacy centered upon 'I'. Whereas *ātman* is not inadequate, it is the whole. The *saṁsārī* desires things and works for the fulfilment of those desires. He feels occasionally happy when some of those desires are fulfilled. At other times, he feels miserable. This is a vicious circle — desire, action, and the impressions created by the fulfilment of desires which breed further desires. One should strive to discover one's own innate nature of fullness, thus becoming free from the misery of pursuing pleasures.

Seventh Verse

In *Dakṣiṇāmūrti Stotram* every verse is like an aphorism (*sūtra*). The entire *śāstra* is presented very briefly and yet in a lucid language. In the earlier verse, we have seen that the glory of *ātman* is covered by the veil of *Māyā*. Now, Śrī Śaṅkara presents a method of discrimination to help us overcome the confusion between the knower and known, this confusion being the basic cause of *saṁsāra*.

बाल्यादिष्वपि जाग्रदादिषु तथा सर्वास्ववस्थास्वपि
व्यावृत्तास्वनुवर्तमानमहमित्यंतःस्फुरंतं सदा ।
स्वात्मानं प्रकटीकरोति भजतां यो भद्रया मुद्रया
तस्मै श्रीगुरुमूर्तये नम इदं श्रीदक्षिणामूर्तये ।। ७ ।।

bālyādiṣvapi jāgradādiṣu tathā sarvāsvavasthāsvapi
vyāvr̥ttāsvanuvartamānamahamityantaḥsphurantaṁ sadā ।
svātmānaṁ prakaṭīkaroti bhajatāṁ yo bhadrayā mudrayā
tasmai śrīgurumūrtaye nama idaṁ śrīdakṣiṇāmūrtaye ॥ 7 ॥

बाल्यादिषु अपि (*bālyādiṣu api*) — childhood, etc., जाग्रदादिषु (*jāgradādiṣu*) — waking state, etc., तथा (*tathā*) — also, सर्वासु (*sarvāsu*) — all, अवस्थासु अपि (*avasthāsu api*) — stages too, व्यावृत्तास्व (*vyāvr̥ttāsva*) — while getting replaced, अनुवर्तमानम् (*anuvartamānam*) — continuously present (pervading), अहं इति (*ahaṁ iti*) — in the form of 'I', अंतः (*antaḥ*) — in the mind, सदा (*sadā*) — always, स्फुरंतं (*sphurantaṁ*) — shining, यः (*yaḥ*) — who, भद्रया (*bhadrayā*) — auspicious or beautiful, मुद्रया (*mudrayā*) — by the configuration of fingers of the hand, भजताम् *bhajatām* — to the devotees, स्वात्मानं (*svātmānaṁ*) — his own *ātman*, प्रकटीकरोति (*prakaṭīkaroti*) — making clear, तस्मै श्रीगुरुमूर्तये नम इदं श्रीदक्षिणामूर्तये (*tasmai śrīgurumūrtaye nama idaṁ śrī-dakṣiṇāmūrtaye*).

All the stages of life such as childhood etc., and states of daily experience such as waking state, etc., come in time and disappear in time. But, during all those varying states, the sense of 'I' is always shining as the innermost essence of every human being. That awareness, the *ātman*, is none other than Lord Dakṣiṇāmūrti. This truth is conveyed by the Lord through a characteristic configuration of fingers of the hand, called *cin-mudrā.* My prostrations unto that Universal Teacher, Lord Dakṣiṇāmūrti, who alone shines in the form of *ātman* in every living being.

Dakṣiṇāmūrti, the Lord of the universe, is the conscious being, *Cetana Puruṣa*. Who is this conscious being? I only know one conscious being and that happens to be me. I am not just a bunch of particles; nor am I a bunch of desires and aspirations. I am a conscious being. I am *Brahman*, if only I can rise above the false limitations imposed upon me by various *upādhis*.

A major portion (nearly 70 per cent) of the body is only water in the form of blood. During blood examination, a small amount of blood is withdrawn into a syringe and placed in a small bottle. When the same blood is in the body, it becomes me and mine. When it is taken out of my body, it is no more me and mine. When I donate the blood, it is collected in a plastic bag and kept in the refrigerator. I do not have the sense of 'I' associated with it. It can go into some other person's body and become the 'I' of that person. You are not the body which is nothing but so much water contained in a bag of skin. You are the indweller of that body, a conscious being, *Cetana Puruṣa*. You can at best say that the body belongs to you. The identification with the material body is the most fundamental and calamitous mistake that a human being commits.

What am I? This is the fundamental question. I have a number of experiences in life. What is their relationship with me? Each experience comes in time and goes in time. Every time an experience comes before me, I identify myself with it. This is what is called *prajñāparādha*, mistake of the intellect. No two experiences are the same. Each experience is different from the other. At lunch or dinner you eat a sweet. Then you eat a hot pickle. If both experiences are the same, you need not have two dishes. What is the relationship between the experiencer and the experience? An experience happens to me. This is another point where we have to modify our understanding. We live our lives by jumping from one experience into another. This is not the truth. The truth is that experience happens to you. You are the central point, the focus, the matrix, *caitanya*, due to which all experiences become possible. It is like waves rising in the ocean one after another. Ocean does not travel from one wave to another. I remain forever the conscious being that I am and various experiences happen to me.

You are the centre of the universe. You are the axis, around which everything including *Īśvara* revolves. The experiencer imparts his reality to the experience. There is no experience outside the experiencer. There is no *sukha* or *duḥkha* outside me. If happiness is available outside as a commodity, it may be neatly packed and marketed. It is not available that way. *Sukha* is not the property of the objects. It is the essential content of the conscious person. As long as a piece of sweet remains outside of me, there is no pleasant experience. It has to be put on my tongue, when sensations of taste buds are conveyed to the brain and integrated to generate a feeling of taste and a sense of well-being rises up from my own inner matrix.

As every experience is different, it follows that every experiencer has to be different. When the boss is angry, the employees wait for him to cool down, before they approach him. When the face of the father is frightful with anger, the children wait till he regains his pleasant countenance. While every experience is different and the experiencer is also different, there is an underlying commonality between different experiences and between different experiencers. I am now happy. I am now unhappy. I am angry. I am composed. I am agitated. The common element among all these experiencers is 'I am'. This 'I am' is the window to the Truth. 'I am' is the crystallised consciousness-cum-existence (*aham asmi sadā bhāmi*).

We have a beautiful name for this 'I am'; it may be called *sākṣī*, the witness. Why do we call it *sākṣī*? In the statements, 'I am happy', 'I am unhappy', etc., what is changing is 'happy', 'unhappy', etc. What remains without change while witnessing all the changes is me, the immutable (*kūṭastha*) *sākṣī*. Witnessing (*sākṣitva*) does not entail any effort. It happens on its own, since it is not an action. It is spontaneous. It is like a lamp spontaneously illuminating everything in its wake. I am not one of those experiences, because I am illuminating all the experiences.

Let us take the four stages of growth in the life of an individual. They are childhood (*bālya*), teenage, middle age and old age. The childhood in everybody's life is a very special experience. Even Rāma regretted that it was over, saying: Alas! gone are those days! Everyone has to say that at sometime or the other. The teenage experience is another interesting experience. It is a carefree life. You have to see a university student to believe it. He declares that the world is in his pocket. Then comes the middle age characterised by a care-worn face. The person is mellowed down by worries, family problems, concern about the future and onset of the signs of ill-health, etc. By then, he must have received a lot of beating in human relationships. Finally old age is altogether a different experience. If the person has matured emotionally by then, he is saved. Otherwise, old age can be a real emotional setback. What to say about the innumerable health problems in old age?

Bālyādiṣu: In each of these stages, the person is identified with that stage of life. All these stages of life belong to the body. All these experiences are transitory. I am neither one of them nor the combination of all. I am the light, which illuminates all of them.

Jāgradādiṣu: Having considered a given human life divided into various stages, now Śrī Śaṅkara talks of a given day in a person's life. The day consists of three states: waking (*jāgrat*), dream (*svapna*) and deep sleep (*suṣupti*) states. What is the waking state? If you think that the waking state consists of various objects, people, liked as well as disliked, earth, heaven, etc.; in other words, that *jāgrat* is a collection of things and people, that object-oriented understanding is incomplete. *Jāgrat* is nothing but a series of subjective experiences, everyone of them appearing to be real and also outside. An object in the waking state is not outside the experience of the subject. Everybody has got his own very special waking state. *Jāgrat* is mostly subjective; it is not objective. I have a set of human relations, memories, etc., which are very personal to me. Nobody shares them with me. Human beings live utterly alone in this world. Nobody shares another's world. Husband lives in the husband's world. Wife lives in the wife's world. There appear to be a few overlaps between them. But, in my opinion, even these overlaps are subjective with reference to both husband and wife. The area of overlap is strictly determined by the subjective prerogative.

In dream we see different things and meet many people. Everyone of these things appear to be different from me, the dream-subject. But, we know that the truth is otherwise. The trees seen in the dream are me; the mountains are me; friends are me; enemies are me. Dream with all its plurality arises out of me and sets in me. It does not exist outside of me. But I am not the dream subject; I am the light that illuminates the entire dream including its subject and its body and senses.

The analogy of dream can be directly extrapolated to the waking state. The most common misconception is that the waking state is real in contrast to the dream. There is absolutely no difference in the circumstances of these two states of experience; everything appears to be real and different from me while that state is on; everything is negated when that state is replaced by another. So, the reality of the status of both the states should be the same. But, due to the beginningless ignorance, waking state seems real and the person is bound by the *saṁsāra* precisely for this reason. If the same dream were to repeat day after day and if it were to persist for a longer duration, then that dream itself would appear real. In fact, some people live in a dream world even in the waking state.

Vedānta throws a challenge before us in concluding that the waking state is as unreal as a dream. In fact, we are all living in a world which is nothing but a dream of rather long duration. We are duped for a lifetime by taking *jāgrat* to be real. Everyday the dream called *jāgrat* repeats itself. The subject of the waking state is as false as the dream subject. The only reality of this mess called life is the awareness which fills every experience, of both waking and dream states, with Existence and Consciousness. That awareness, which is not limited by the mental categories of time and space, is the *ātman* which is *Brahman*.

In deep sleep (*suṣupti*), we experience relative nothingness with respect to what all we have experienced in the other two states. It is like closing down the window of light to the senses. None of the events is registered, because the mind, which has projected a world without the help of sense-organs in the dream state, is now resolved completely in its source, the *ātman*. Deep sleep is a third kind of experience. The matrix of all these states is the *ātman*. It is called *turiīya* (the fourth) as it is taken up for discussion after the three states. But it is not one more state; it is the stateless Existence-Light that is in and through all the states imparting its own Reality and Light of Consciousness to them.

Vyāvr̥ttāsu anuvartamānam. *Ātman* is the underlying matrix which does not change in this perennial flow of different experiences. There is a law in Vedānta. All changes take place against a changeless background. Many experiences come and go (*vyāvr̥ttāsu*). Every time we take a particular experience to be true, only to be proved false soon. *Ātman* is the only reality of all these experiences. Lord Śrī Kr̥ṣṇa lived simultaneously with eight wives. He appeared to belong exclusively to each one of them; in reality He belonged to none.

The idea is not to condemn any particular state or experience. We should not be carried away by emotions. Emotions could be good but they could deceive us. We have to play the roles enjoined upon us, without getting attached to them beyond a point. In life, we should step aside, as it were, from the field of experiences and try to be a witness to everything that happens before us, never identifying with an experience. The witnessing attitude is the *mahāmantra* and *mahāsiddhi*. This is the greatest Yoga, the *ātma-yoga*. There is no other solution for the problems of *saṁsāra*. *Ātma-yoga* is remaining a witness, which is described by sages as the window to the Supreme Reality. Śrī Śaṅkara quite often presents the *ātman* as the *sakala buddhipratyaya sākṣī*.

Ahamityantaḥsphurantaṁ sadā: The experiences of a human being change continuously; but, 'I am' is common to all the experiences. This 'I am' is nothing but the Supreme Reality reflected in the *antaḥkaraṇa*. How many 'I am's are there in this world? Infinite. It is like one Sun reflecting in a billion dew-drops. If you come down from the level of the reflection and become one with whatever is perceived and illuminated by the reflection, there is no hope. One has to step aside from the modifications of the mind and stay with 'I am' to gain liberation from bondage. The supreme truth, Dakṣiṇāmūrti, is in the form of *ātman* in every living being. The essential content of 'I am' is Dakṣiṇāmūrti, the *Paramātman*. This is what Bhagavān says in the *Gītā* (10-20).

अहमात्मा गुडाकेश सर्वभूताशयस्थितः ।

ahamātmā guḍākeśa sarvabhūtāśayasthitaḥ ।

O Conqueror of ignorance, I am the *ātman* obtaining in the minds of all living beings.

This truth is beautifully conveyed by Dakṣiṇāmūrti by

showing the *jñāna-mudrā* with the right hand, *svātmānaṁ prakaṭīkaroti bhajatāṁ yo bhadrayā mudrayā*. While teaching the *Gītā*, Lord Śrī Kṛṣṇa also shows the same *mudrā*.

> ज्ञानमुद्राय कृष्णाय गीतामृतदुहे नमः ।
> *jñānamudrāya kṛṣṇāya gītāmṛtaduhe namaḥ* ।
>
> My salutations unto the Lord Śrī Kṛṣṇa, who was showing the *jñāna-mudrā* with his hand, while milking the nectar of *Gītā* from the cow of Upaniṣads.

The *mudrā*s (specific configurations of fingers and hands) are very much characteristic to the Hindu mode of worship. They are to be seen in the day-to-day life as body language. Animals are well known to use body language. Human beings also use body language to a less extent as they are endowed with speech. Even the *devatā* worshipped by us uses them, since the *devatā* maintains a stony silence. The Lord speaks through the *mudrā*s. The famous form of Lord Veṅkaṭeśvara has two *mudrā*s, *abhaya-mudrā* and *varada-mudrā*. People are mainly interested in these two *mudrā*s alone. Majority of the people are not very keen about *jñāna-mudrā*.

The human being is essentially insecure due to his identification with the body. He is always burdened with various concerns and fears; fear of the future, endless fear of one's own economic strength, etc. Also, the human being is a bundle of desires, small and big, for the same reason. The *devatā* has to address these two things; otherwise the *devatā* may not be worshipped at all. Vedānta is not against this or anything else for that matter. Vedānta validates and reconciles all modes of worship. But Vedānta advises us to rise above the level of desires and fears as soon as we can. Lord Veṅkaṭeśvara has one more *mudrā*, the *jñāna-mudrā*, which he has reserved for the time being. He, as

Dakṣiṇāmūrti, shows it to guide the qualified person.

The devotees of Lord Dakṣiṇāmūrti do not implore him for things of this world or the other. They approach him for overcoming the limitations of desires and fears by the knowledge of *ātman*. Thus the *abhaya-* and *varada-mudrā*s are transformed into *jñāna-mudrā*. A *mudrā*, like any body language, becomes meaningful only when the other person understands its significance. It is a very special kind of teaching. What about the people who don't understand the meaning of that *mudrā*? *Mudrā* is translated into teaching by the *ācārya*. This *mudrā* is shown to the devotees who worship Dakṣiṇāmūrti with a desire to address and solve the fundamental problem of fear and desire. These devotees are not interested in temporary solutions for the problem of *saṁsāra*, the life of a limited being.

There are four kinds of devotees: a devotee in distress (*ārta*), a devotee ambitious of achieving something (*arthārthī*), a devotee desirous of knowledge of *ātman* (*jijñāsu*), and the devotee endowed with that knowledge (*jñānī*). Bhagavān reassures a devotee in distress with *abhaya-mudrā*. He encourages the ambitious (in the right path) devotee with *varada-mudrā*. *Jñāna-mudrā* is reserved for a *jijñāsu*. For a *jñānī*, no *mudrā* is required, because he is no different from *Īśvara* himself. This wonderful classification of devotees is presented by Bhagavān in the *Gītā* as follows:

चतुर्विधा भजंते मां जनास्सुकृतिनोऽर्जुन ।
आर्तो जिज्ञासुरर्थार्थी ज्ञानी च भरतर्षभ ।। (७-१६)
उदारास्सर्व एवैते ज्ञानी त्वात्मैव मे मतम् । (७-१८)

caturvidhā bhajante māṁ janāssukṛtino'rjuna ।
ārto jijñāsurarthārthī jñānī ca bharatarṣabha ।। (7-16)
udārāssarva evaite jñānī tvātmaiva me matam । (7-18)

The people, given to good actions, who worship me are four-fold, O Arjuna, . . . the one in distress, the one who wants security and pleasure, the one who wishes to know (me), and the one who knows (me), O foremost in the family of Bharata.

All these indeed are exalted, but the one who knows (me) is myself alone.

This *jñāna-mudrā* is very auspicious, *bhadrā*. What is the auspiciousness of this *mudrā*? There was a gentleman who was afraid of demons, whenever he was alone in a dark or semi-dark room. The demon was obviously his own mental projection. It exists in his thoughts alone, and thoughts in turn have their existence in the ocean of consciousness, which is *ātman*. Thus, the demon is none other than the *ātman*. The mind forms its own notions based on its store of *vāsanā*s, takes them to be real and then it is afraid of them. When this was explained to that gentleman, his problem of fear was solved. Knowledge removes fear. *Ātma-jñāna* is a panacea for all kinds of fears. Knowledge keeps the undesirable desires away. There are many auspicious things and deeds, but knowledge of *ātman* tops them all. So, *jñāna-mudrā* includes all other *mudrā*s in itself. Bhagavān described the glory of knowledge in the *Gītā* as follows:

सर्वं कर्माखिलं पार्थ ज्ञाने परिसमाप्यते । (४-३३)
न हि ज्ञानेन सदृशं पवित्रमिह विद्यते । (४-३८)

sarvam karmākhilam pārtha jñāne parisamāpyate । (4-33)
na hi jñānena sadṛśaṁ pavitramiha vidyate । (4-38)

All action, in its entirety, O Pārtha, is resolved in knowledge.

Therefore, in this world, there is no purifier equivalent to knowledge.

The significance of this *mudrā* is as follows: The index finger represents the individual, *jīva*. We use this finger alone to point at another person. The other three fingers are always associated with the index finger. These four fingers get their strength from the thumb. Before independence, Dhaka muslin cloth was considered superior to the Manchester cloth. To avoid competition from the former, it is said that the British have cut down the thumbs of the Dhaka weavers. This is exactly what Droṇācārya did to Ekalavya. The aim was to destroy the extra-ordinary skill of these people. They did not resort to cutting the entire hand to fulfil their aim. That would spill unnecessary blood. This shows the significance of the thumb in all the jobs done with hands. Weight lifters will not be able to lift the same weight if the thumb is not brought into play. As an organ of action, hand derives its strength from the thumb. That strength is the *kriyā-śakti*, which is one of the manifestations of *Īśvara*.

There is a two-fold manifestation of *Īśvara* in this body; one is the power of knowledge, *jñāna-śakti,* expressed through the five sense-organs, mind, intellect and memory. And the other is the life force, *kriyā-śakti*, expressed through exhalation and inhalation, organs of action, digestive power, blood flow, heart beat, etc. All voluntary and involuntary actions of the body are the expressions of this *kriyā-śakti* alone. We can reach the source, *Īśvara,* through any one of these manifestations by backward integration, either through *prāṇāyāma* or *dhyāna*. Thus, in the language of *mudrā,* thumb stands for *Īśvara*.

The other three fingers represent the world (macrocosm) or the body-mind-sense complex (microcosm). They are created from the *prakṛti* which is made up of three *guṇa*s, namely, *sattva*, *rajas* and *tamas*. The three fingers stand for these three *guṇa*s. Or, simply they stand for the body, senses and the mind. They may even represent the gross (*sthūla*) body, the subtle (*sūkṣma*) body and the causal (*kāraṇa*) body of the individual.

The index finger is placed in such a way that it can associate either with the three fingers on one side or with the thumb on the other side. In the same way, the person can go all out into the world and enjoy the pleasures of the world; or, having recognised the folly of pleasure-seeking, he may try to go back to his source, the *Brahmātman*. The individual consists of the body, mind, and the *ātman*. The person, located in the mind, can either identify himself with the insentient body due to ignorance; or know and merge with his own essential nature, the *ātman*. *Jīvatva*, the status of being a *jīva*, is nothing but a notion created by the mind. There is nothing like an entity called *jīva*.

In the *jñāna-mudrā*, the index finger touches the thumb forming a circle, implying the essence of the teaching as: O *jīva*! Stay in association with *Īśvara*; worship *Īśvara* or know and abide in *ātman*. Don't be dissociated from your own source, namely, *Īśvara*. Don't be a beggar of happiness at the door of the unreal world. We have to keep the worldly thoughts away to the extent possible and try to find our equation with *Īśvara*. Our real home is not the world. *Īśvara* is the real abode of *jīva*. The circle formed by the index finger with the thumb signifies the essential non-difference between *Īśvara* and *jīva*.

People worship *Īśvara* for the fulfilment of their desires. This kind of worship is called *kāmya-karma*. This kind of worship is very much a part of Vedic teaching, since the human aspirations are taken into account in the *vaidika dharma*. But, Vedānta in general and the *Gītā* in particular, does not recommend this kind of worship. These scriptures recommend a cautious approach towards pleasures of the world, because here in Vedānta, the ultimate goal of human endeavour is to gain the knowledge of *ātman*. The body, mind and the senses are put to judicial use without losing sight of the ultimate goal.

Jīvatva is a status ascribed to *Brahman* due to ignorance. *Īśvaratva* is another status ascribed to the same *Brahman* from the standpoint of being worshipped by devotees. Thus, the One *Brahman* acquires different names, when viewed from the standpoint of *upādhi*s. *Brahman* from the standpoint of creation is called *Īśvara*. When *Brahman* expresses in the original seed of this universe called *mahat*, it is called *hiraṇyagarbha*. Similarly from the standpoint of the gross physical world, *Brahman* is called *virāṭ* and from the standpoint of the universal energy, *Brahman* is called *sūtrātman*.

The same *Brahman* when manifesting through the *upādhi* of a human body is called *jīva*, and when manifesting through the *upādhi* of an ant is called ant. He is called Indra, Varuṇa, etc., with different *upādhi*s. *Ekam sat viprā bahudhā vadanti* (The Reality is one. The wise call It with various names). The same *Brahman* is called Lakṣmī through the *upādhi* of wealth, Sarasvatī through the *upādhi* of knowledge, Viṣṇu with respect to sustenance and protection of the universe, and Rudra from the standpoint of annihilation of the universe. The same *Brahman* is called Śiva with respect to auspiciousness. Ornaments are many; but gold is one. *Upādhi*s are innumerable; but *Brahman* is one and only One. One such name for *Brahman* is *jīva*. The *upādhi* is different but not the essential content, *dhātu*. From the existence standpoint, the Supreme Reality is called *Brahman*, and from the awareness standpoint, the same Reality is called *ātman*. The supreme goal of human life is *ānanda*, happiness. From the standpoint of *ānanda*, happiness, we call it *ananta*. *Satyam jñānamanantam brahma* (*Brahman* is Existence-Awareness-Absolute).

The separation between *jīva* and *Īśvara* is like the separation between the necklace and gold, or between the wave and water. We have been committed to our notion of being a small person. That smallness is not the property of the *ātman* or *caitanya*, but it is the property of the *upādhi*. This fact is usually ignored. We gradually develop a love for this ignorance. It is like a slave loving his slavery. That is how the mind functions. A prisoner develops some attachment to his cell. So also we develop an attachment for *jīvatva*. The *jñāna-mudrā* is an exhortation to us by *Īśvara* to come out of this bondage. We should try to relate to *Īśvara* with a view to understand our essential identity with *Īśvara*.

We have to transcend the body by keeping the body healthy. If it is ill, it cries for help and we get stuck with it. In the same way, unless the mind is pure, we cannot go beyond the bondage caused by the mind. Purification of mind implies dilution of likes and dislikes. Such a person can relate with *Īśvara* spontaneously without bringing desires into the picture. Such a person gradually grows, by the grace of *Īśvara*, into the Cosmic consciousness of his oneness with *Īśvara*. In the life of such a seeker, the lifestyle, the roles played by the person, the company he keeps, the values he follows in day-to-day life, etc., are conducive to such a vision.

Eighth Verse

In this eighth verse, Śrī Śaṅkara reduces the universal human experiences into certain fundamental categories and expounds the phenomenal nature of the universe. It is the glory of Śrī Śaṅkara that he unequivocally recognises the plurality of the universe as unreal and that it is a product of ignorance. The fragmentary world vision of an ignorant person is beautifully presented by Śrī Śaṅkara in this verse.

विश्वं पश्यति कार्यकारणतया स्वस्वामिसंबंधतः
शिष्याचार्यतया तथैव पितृपुत्राद्यात्मना भेदतः ।
स्वप्ने जाग्रति वा य एष पुरुषो मायापरिभ्रामितः
तस्मै श्रीगुरुमूर्तये नम इदं श्रीदक्षिणामूर्तये ।। ८ ।।

viśvaṁ paśyati kāryakāraṇatayā svasvāmisam-bandhataḥ
śiṣyācāryatayā tathaiva pitṛputrādyātmanā bhedataḥ ।
svapne jāgrati vā ya eṣa puruṣo māyāparibhrāmitaḥ
tasmai śrīgurumūrtaye nama idaṁ śrīdakṣiṇā-mūrtaye ।। 8 ।।

यः (*yaḥ*) — who, एषः (*eṣaḥ*) — this, पुरुषः (*puruṣaḥ*) — person, मायापरिभ्रामितः (*māyāparibhrāmitaḥ*) — being completely deluded by *māyā*, स्वप्ने (*svapne*) — in the dream, वा (*vā*) — or, जाग्रति (*jāgrati*) — in the wakeful state, विश्वं (*viśvam*) — the world, कार्यकारणतया (*kāryakāraṇatayā*) — in terms of cause and effect,

स्वस्वामिसंबंधतः (*svasvāmisambandhataḥ*) — in terms of the relationship between the owned and the owner, शिष्याचार्यतया (*śiṣyācāryatayā*) — in terms of the student and the teacher, तथैव (*tathaiva*) — in the same way, पितृपुत्राद्यात्मना (*pitṛputrādyātmanā*) — in terms of the father and the son etc., भेदतः (*bhedataḥ*) — in terms of division, पश्यति (*paśyati*) — sees, तस्मै श्रीगुरुमूर्तये नम इदं श्रीदक्षिणामूर्तये (*tasmai śrīgurumūrtaye nama idaṁ śrīdakṣiṇāmūrtaye*).

This person sees the world, in both waking and dream states in plurality, divided into cause and effect, owner and the owned, student and teacher, son and father, etc. He does so due to the all-round delusion of *Māyā*. But he is no different from Lord Dakṣiṇāmūrti, the Universal teacher. My salutations unto Him.

Viśvaṁ paśyati: The person sees the world and experiences it. How? *Bhedataḥ paśyati*. We see division and plurality everywhere. There is nothing wrong with it. After all, it is the plurality that is visible. But, what the eyes see may not be the truth always. For example, I see the Sun rising in the east and setting in the west. But the truth is altogether different. We see a patch of blue colour in the sky. But we should not straight away conclude that the space is blue in colour. Space can never be blue. A wall or a piece of cloth or an object may have colour, but not space. Only a material object with parts can have colour as a quality. But space is partless. Eye as a sense-organ has many limitations. It can see objects correctly only when they are within a certain range. Sometimes the eyesight needs a correction. The deep-rooted impressions of the mind influence quite often what the eyes see. Therefore the notion that what we see is true is wrong. Whatever we may see cannot be accepted as real without further inquiry. This understanding is the starting point for the seeker in his journey towards Truth.

Rationalists demand that *Īśvara* should be visible before they accept Him. If *Īśvara* can be shown, that goes against the definition of *Īśvara*. Whatever is visible to the eyes cannot be *Īśvara*. The contention that whatever is visible is real does not stand scrutiny at all. *Īśvara* is the substratum of this universe. It is very clear to a discerning eye that there is a very high degree of order and symmetry in the entire universe. Therefore, a universe which is thus intelligently put together presupposes a sentient cause.

Science and Vedānta operate on the basis of the same principle of negation (*apavāda*). They both negate our visual experiences as unreal. I see this water in the cup as a single unit. But, science proves that it is a collection of particles. Our idea of the Sun rising and setting is proved wrong by the science. We see what the eyes show, and also see more than that. If the plurality experienced by the sense-organs were to be real, then we would not need any science or *śāstra* at all. Science and *śāstra* investigate this plurality, and show us the underlying unity. That is their purpose. Their purpose is not just to validate whatever we see or experience as real.

We look at this world from the standpoint of a framework that is already fixed in the mind: the framework of time, space and causality. Let us first look into the cause-effect division. Take the example of a necklace and gold. They are supposed to be two different things. There is a school of thought, called Nyāya (logic), which maintains that the cause and effect are different; that the effect arises (*ārabhyate*) out of the cause at a given moment. This school is called *ārambhavāda*. In this school, an elaborate logic is spun around a common misunderstanding of cause-effect division. The basic truth that the effect is not an independent entity and that it depends upon the cause for its existence is ignored. The necklace is nothing more than a particular form in which the gold itself is appearing before us. We name it and then take it to be real as it has a name also.

When we are looking at a necklace, there is just one object before us, though there may be two things in the mind, namely, necklace and gold. Based on this mental construct, we call one of them as cause and the other as effect. Mind is then at rest, since it has once again indulged in its favourite pastime of dividing where there is no division. I see only one object; not two. The necklace and gold are not two things like a cow and a horse. We do not have two things; we have just two names. We should reorganise our process of thinking. We take it for granted that there are independent objects in this universe. We ignore the fact that there is no object independent of time and space. An object is invariably associated with time and space. All the three, namely, time, space and object, arise together and set together. Therefore, the universe consists of events rather than objects.

The idea of causation arises in the mind due to the succession of events. An event happens in zero time. It is stored in the memory of the mind. Another event happens after a length of time. Mind connects both these events and concludes that the former is the cause of the latter. In this conclusion, the event is once again mistakenly taken for an object. This is the psychology underlying the great Nyāya *śāstra*. I have a gold biscuit in my hand now. This is one event. Later I have a necklace in my hand. This is the second event. The gold biscuit is the initial event and the necklace is the latter event. Therefore I say the necklace is the effect, and the gold biscuit is the cause. Thus, we have a distorted vision of the *kārya-kāraṇa* division in place and it binds us to this *saṁsāra*. If we care to see the truth that past and present are only mental categories, and that both are superimpositions on the eternal undivided awareness, what will happen to this cause-effect division? It will collapse like a pack of cards.

In this universe, every event is influenced by and connected to every other event. To say one particular event is the cause of another event is a superficiality. The necklace is caused not only by gold but also by innumerable events like the sunrise, the birth of the goldsmith, the law of gravity, presence of oxygen in the air, etc. In this world, no event happens in isolation or without influencing every other event. According to Newton's third law, for every action, there is a reaction. Suppose you put one step forward. The earth moves a small fraction of a distance in the opposite direction. Until the earth is pushed behind, you cannot move one step ahead. When the earth is disturbed a little, every planet connected to the earth through the law of gravitation is in turn disturbed. It is like disturbing a magnet surrounded by iron filings. All the iron filings experience a change in the magnetic field. Thus, while every event, small or big, influences every other event, what kind of cause-effect relationship are we talking about? It is the pastime of the mind to search for causes at every occasion. In reality, there is only one cause. That is *Brahman*. This vision of the universe as an apparition in *Brahman* releases the human being from the bondage of this plurality.

In our day-to-day life, we extend this cause-effect relation to the living beings also. Śrī Śaṅkara refers to it in the phrase *pitṛputrādyātmanā*. We normally understand that father is the cause of the son. The parents give birth to a child as a part of the scheme called universe. It grows and manifests its own *prārabdha* in life. Parents assume that they are responsible for that life. But Śrī Śaṅkara has a different vision about it.

का ते कांता कस्ते पुत्रस्संसारोऽयमतीव विचित्रः ।
कस्य त्वं कः कुत आयातस्तत्त्वं चिंतय यदिदं भ्रातः ।।
— मोहमुद्गरः, ८

kā te kāntā kaste putrassaṁsāro'yamatīva vicitraḥ ।
kasya tvaṁ kaḥ kuta āyātastattvaṁ cintaya yadidaṁ bhrātaḥ ।। — *Mohamudgaraḥ*, 8

Who is your wife (husband)? Who is your son (daughter)? This life of a limited being is indeed very baffling. To whom do you belong? Who are you? Wherefrom did you come? Dear brother, understand your essential truth.

In the *Chāndogya Upaniṣad*, there is a section called *pañcāgni vidyā*. The piligrimage of a virtuous *jīva* is described in that *vidyā* (*upāsanā*). He performed many rituals enjoined by the Veda, and attained the heavens. He enjoyed his stay there for a length of time till his *puṇya* was almost exhausted. *Kṣīṇe puṇye martyalokaṁ viśanti*; the *jīva* has to return to this world after his virtue is exhausted. He started his journey back to this earth to take birth as a human being, so that he can earn more *puṇya* and then again go to heavens. He enters from the interstellar space in a subtle form into the rain-bearing clouds. As the rain falls on the ground, he enters into the soil through the rain waters. Each stage in this journey is allegorically presented as a fire. It is well known that fire predominates in the Vedic worship. It is the physical *agni* where you offer oblations or *upāsanā-agni* which you meditate upon or the fire of knowledge (*jñānāgni*) which destroys the bondage of *karma*. The plants absorb the ground water through their roots. Now, the *jīva* obtains in the nutrition principles of a plant, like grains, pulses, vegetables or fruits. His remaining *puṇya* directs the events in such a way that this food is eaten by a male. Now the *jīva* is in the blood of that person. Then he enters into the womb of a woman and takes birth in time. Thus the *jīva* has passed through five stages, each a fire. Now the question is : Who is the father of this *jīva*? The so-called father is at the most one-fifth of a father. Even that is doubtful, since his volition is totally absent in the entire sequence of events. When I go to New York, I transit through two airports, one at Bombay and another at London. Thus, I have two fathers, the airports at Bombay and London. Is it so?

A stage in the journey cannot acquire the status of a cause. *Jīva* continues to exist in one form or other, as determined by his own *karma*. So this *pitṛputrā bheda* is false. There is no *pitā* and there is no *putra*. All are *jīva*s and all are *Brahman*. In the flow of time, the birth of one *jīva* precedes that of another. This is taken as the basis of parenthood. If we want to have some working relationship for running the *saṁsāra*, it is all right. But if anybody thinks that the father-son relationship is the ultimate truth and the division between the father and son is very real, then he is mistaken. The parenthood is a superimposition on the person, originating from the family and from the society. *Śāstra*s validate it so that the person performs his duty towards the children. More than that, there is no absolute parenthood for *ātman*. The teaching is that there are different people, but there is no division.

We are all playing different roles on this stage of the world. One plays the role of a father and another that of a son in a movie-like life. Suppose I had a dream. Certain parts of the dream are very lovable to me. And certain other parts are a nightmare to me. I cannot complain about them. Whatever is lovable to me in the dream is as much unreal as the nightmare in the dream. Dream is not a problem. But developing likes and dislikes about the things in the dream is the real problem.

Life is nothing but a bundle of innumerable events and the memory of those events makes me a person. There is nothing more to the 'person' than the memory of the mind or history. *Svasvāmīsambandhataḥ*: I am the *svāmī*, the master and he is the servant. In a certain situation, a person is working as a servant. A favourable *karma* put me in the place of a master. I may play the role of the master, and extract work from the servant. To that extent it is alright. But, if I develop superiority complex that I am the master and he is the servant, it is wrong. There is no servant and there is no master in this world. All are human beings. One human being is playing the role of a servant; another that of a master. Nobody is a born-master or a born-servant. We should be aware of the fact that this 'master-hood' and 'servant-hood' are very ephemeral states and even when they are on, they are nothing more than notions. This understanding does not adversely affect master-servant relationship. He stays in his place, and I in mine. He does his work, and I do mine. A benevolent master is doing a service not only to the servant, but also to himself. If the master role goes to the head, *ahaṅkāra* (egotism) grows. The *ahaṅkāra*, the *mānitva* (sense of superiority) is a very great obstacle in the path of Truth. In the 13th chapter of the *Gītā*, an entire value system is presented by Bhagavān for the guidance of seekers. The list of values starts very significantly with *amānitva* (lack of superiority or ego problem).

One of the servers in a hotel has saved money day after day and purchased the same hotel from the owner. The owner was compelled to sell the hotel due to financial difficulties but he was very happy to sell it to one of his own servers. The notion that I am a master on a permanent basis is wrong.

It does not do any good to the psychology of the person. This principle applies even to the division between the devotee and the Lord. The devotee surrenders before the Lord. He looks upon himself as *dāsa* (servant) before *Īśvara*. But this is only for the present. He understands that he will eventually gain knowledge and become one with *Īśvara* by knowledge. We worship the Lord only to transcend this division between us and the Lord by realising our essential oneness with the Lord. The kind of devotion which considers that any talk of unity is blasphemous and believes that the division between *Īśvara* and *jīva* is eternal is an aberration of *dharma* that gained currency in later times.

The world in which a person lives hangs entirely on the thread of his memory. It is altogether based on the framework of a few mental categories and a few details completely within that structure. The basic mental categories are three in number: time, space and causation. We live in a prison cell of these three walls erected by our minds. It is very much separated from the Reality. This world vision is at the base of all our trials and tribulations. On the other hand, in the *jñānī*'s world, there is that one Reality, the *ātman*. Everything else is unreal. *Sarvaṁ khalvidaṁ brahma*. In the heart of a *jñānī*, there is only one emotion, namely, a love which does not have an agenda and which demands nothing in return.

As such there is nothing wrong in seeing different things. Different things are seen, but separation is not the fact. Objects as perceived by sense-organs and mind are many, but matter is one. I am not talking of matter from the point of a view of a materialist. By matter, I mean *vastu*. In Vedānta we talk of *vastu*. There is only one *vastu* in this universe and that *vastu* is the substratum of this entire universe. That *vastu* is variously known as *Īśvara*, God, Viṣṇu, Śiva, Durgā, Divine Being, *ātman* or *Brahman*. Duality is an appearance and the non-dual *Brahman* is the Reality.

There are two kinds of creation: the cosmic (*Īśvara sṛṣṭi*) and the personal (*jīva sṛṣṭi*). The former consists of the sun, the moon, the five great elements, namely, the earth, waters, fire, air and space; it consists of the Laws of Nature like the law of gravitation; it has a variety of people, animals, birds and other living beings in it. We don't live in that kind of a world, in that Cosmic consciousness. We are accustomed to take that world for granted from the childhood itself. We live in a world, which is entirely invented by the mind for us. The subjective world is entirely dominated and populated by personal likes and dislikes. Even if there is the sun or the moon in that world, they are there only because they are somehow connected with the structure of *rāga* and *dveṣa*. I have to go and meet some body in the morning. In that sense, the sunrise becomes relevant to me. Otherwise, I don't care for the sun or sunrise. I fall down and I am hurt. That is how I understand the law of gravity. Otherwise, I don't care for the law of gravity. This mind has got a peculiar knack of creating things and then taking them to be real.

Children, especially small girls, often play a very interesting game. One of the children plays mother. She has a good collection of toy utensils. The mother puts a little sand in one of the utensils. It is supposed to be rice. She may even put real rice, if she can get hold of some without the knowledge of the real-life mother. She adds a little water and goes through all the motions of cooking it. In a little while, the cooking is supposedly completed. Then the mother distributes the imaginary food to the other children, who are supposed to be her sons and daughters. Everyone of them pretends to eat the food. They take part in that play with all seriousness. Once I observed this play without their knowledge. I was amused by the fact that they take the play to be very real. I suppose the games like cricket, etc., played by the professional players are same as this game of the children, as far as reality situation is concerned. If you agree with me here, then you can readily appreciate that the life we lead is also as imaginary as that game of the children. The mind creates every situation and takes it to be real. I may sound like a nihilist or a pessimist. In Vedānta however, we do not care for labels like optimism and pessimism; we investigate life with a view to know the truth, the entire truth and nothing but the truth. As *jijñāsu*s we should be ready to face difficulties in our search for truth.

Māyāparibhrāmitaḥ: A silk worm releases saliva which dries up instantly to give a silk thread. It builds the cocoon with that thread around itself; it lives in it for a while, and finally meets its end within that silky case. Similarly, our mind spins a web of a subjective world due to ignorance. We live like prisoners in it and finally die in it. A person who takes the dream to be real becomes a slave to that dream. People are afraid of nightmares. Where is this nightmare? It is the creation of the mind. One who assumes it to be real is frightened by it.

A *jñānī*'s world is essentially the creation of *Īśvara*. Life and light should not contradict each other. For example, it is well known that consumption of alcohol is bad for health. If somebody keeps the alcohol away in life, then there is a correlation between the life and the knowledge. But, if a person cannot keep away from it, then his life is opposed to his knowledge. Life in conflict with reality pulls the person down. We want peace of mind. But we work for the opposite. We want peace in the society. But we work for the war. We want rest, but work for restlessness. We want health and of course, we work against health. This is *Māyā*.

The things and people around us are continuously changing. But the thraldom of *Māyā* is so powerful, that we take all of them to be real. Till yesterday I took so many things to be real. This morning I found them to be false. How many times the things loved by us have come to naught? How many times the dream has collapsed? Yet we are not ready to accept the reality. I am not ready to see the dream as a dream. I have a mental make-up, which is afraid of truth. It has developed a vested interest in its own falsehood. This is *Māyā*. Like Goebbels, we repeat an untruth ten times and then believe it to be the truth.

We take it that the mind is in the body and the *ātman* or awareness is in the mind. But, the truth is contrary to it. The body is nothing but a notion that exists in the mind. The *prāṇa-śakti* (vital forces), all the modifications of the mind such as feelings, etc., the intellect and all its modifications like the *kartṛtva,* etc., and the *ahaṅkāra*, I-sense, that ego around which the notion of enjoyership (*bhoktṛtva*) is centred . . . everyone of these modifications appears and exists in the consciousness. In a movie, all the characters, their physical bodies and their actions, their sentiments like valour, fright (*nava rasa*s) — everyone of them appears on the background of one light, which is their truth. Similarly, the human being, male or female, his/her body, the number of roles played by him/her like father/mother, son/daughter, etc., the various stages in life, emotional upheavals, trials and tribulations, occasions of joy . . . everyone of them is appearing on the matrix of awareness which is the light of the person's life. It is the ego around which this entire dream is centered. We ignore that *ātman* by giving reality to a dream. The treasure is always in our own backyard but we are ignorant of it. This is *Māyā*.

We live a life burdened with anxiety, sorrow, hurt and

regret. It is like an old man travelling in a train while keeping his luggage on the head. We live with a sense of persecution. 'Why me?' is our perennial complaint. We carry a number of people in the mind. Those people are busy with their lives but we carry them inside. Sometimes we may even think that they cannot live without us. People insure their life. The underlying logic is that the family will be helpless if the person dies. In a limited economic sense, this is quite correct. But, if the idea is taken too seriously, then it is wrong. Who has taken care of the person when he was in mother's womb? Money will not save a person. It helps us to purchase a few things. It gives economic elbowroom. We tend to give more value to things in life than they really have, and in the process we lose our direction. This is *Māyā*.

Our situation is beautifully illustrated by a story in the *Bṛhadāraṇyaka Upaniṣad Bhāṣya* of Śrī Śaṅkara. A prince was kidnapped in the childhood by some dacoits. The child was brought up by them in their hideout. In course of time, he became a dacoit in his own right. But one day he was caught and brought into the court of the king. The minister recognised the young dacoit as the prince who was kidnapped long back. What that dacoit should do to become the prince? He has to realise his identity with the prince and stop acting like a thief. He should live like a prince, as he is already one. In the same way, the *sat-cit-ānanda ātman* has, as though, became a *saṁsārin* due to the ignorance of one's own real nature. This is *Māyā*.

Puruṣaḥ māyāparibhrāmitaḥ : The human being is confused about some of the most important things of life. He has many notions about himself, about the world around him, and about the *Īśvara* that he worships. These notions are not the result of any investigation, or study of scriptures, or consultation with wise people (*mahātmā*s). We inherit these notions through the parents, through the members of the household, and through the society. Even the education in colleges and universities does not help us much to improve the situation. And, of course, one's own reservoir of *karma* and *ajñāna* from times immemorial is there. Therefore we are born into the *saṁsāra*. It is not that a child is born and then after a length of time *saṁsāra* comes in. It is like a fish born into the ocean. Therefore we are constantly struggling and going in circles (*paribhramaṇa*) in life.

This *paribhramaṇa* can be understood in many ways. We are caught in an endless cycle of births and deaths. Śrī Śaṅkara describes this cycle elsewhere as follows:

पुनरपि जननं पुनरपि मरणं पुनरपि जननीजठरे शयनम् ।
इह संसारे बहुदुस्तारे कृपयाऽपारे पाहि मुरारे ।।

— *मोहमुद्गरः*, २१

punarapi jananaṁ punarapi maraṇaṁ punarapi jananījaṭhare śayanam ।
iha saṁsāre bahudustāre kṛpayā'pāre pāhi murāre ।।

— *Mohamudgaraḥ*, 21

The ignorant *jīva* takes birth again; dies again and again enters and stays in the womb of the mother. This ocean of *saṁsāra* has no end; it is very difficult to cross. O Lord Murāri (one who destroyed the demon Mura), please protect me.

Lord Śrī Kṛṣṇa also mentions about this cycle in the *Gītā*.

जातस्य हि ध्रुवो मृत्युर्ध्रुवं जन्म मृतस्य च । (२-२७)
jātasya hi dhruvo mṛtyurdhruvaṁ janma mṛtasya ca ।।(2-27)

For that which is born, death is certain; and for that which is dead, birth is certain.

Even in a given span of life, sometimes, the wheel of fortune puts you in a higher position only to pull you down the next moment.

Śrī Śaṅkara has got one more *paribhramaṇa* in mind. This *bhramaṇa* is talked about in Vedānta alone. The word *bhrānti* (delusion) is quite popular in Vedāntic lore. Both these words are indeed synonymous. What is this *bhramaṇa*? I am *ātman,* the light, which illuminates the ego, intellect, mind, sense-organs, the physical body and the entire universe appearing before this body-mind-sense complex. This *ātman* is shining as the innermost reality of all life forms. It is like the electricity lighting up a city of million lights, or the Sun reflecting in a billion dew drops or wavelets.

That light of awareness is reflected in this *antaḥkaraṇa* like even the Sun is reflected in a mirror. The *antaḥkaraṇa* is a combination of five subtle great elements. The mirror is silica and sand is also silica. The mirror reflects the Sun, but not the sand. Similarly the mind is made up of five elements and the entire insentient world including the gross body is also made up of five elements. But the latter cannot reflect the *ātman* the way mind does, since mind is subtle. When thus the mind reflects *ātman,* it becomes the witness, *sākṣī* of everything starting from ego down to the world outside.

The apparent downfall of the *ātman* has already started. If you can remain as pure *sākṣī* without getting involved with what is witnessed, you are almost liberated. A person, who can remain a *sākṣī* of the three states of consciousness, viz., waking, dream, and deep sleep states, *avasthātraya sākṣī*, is a liberated soul. For him there is no *saṁsāra,* because *Īśvara* will shower his blessing, *anugraha*, upon him. The person has done his part of the job. The rest of it is to be done by *Īśvara* and it will be done.

But let us now discuss the downward journey, the *bhramaṇa*. So the *sarvavyāpaka akhaṇḍa caitanya*, the awareness which is the substratum for the entire universe which is shining in every living being as the I-sense, that non-dual *Brahman*, has now as though become the witness. The witness is unreal as witness, since what is witnessed (*sākṣya*) is unreal. But, the witness is real being the reflection of the Supreme Reality. Don't forget 'as though'. Suppose the Supreme Reality has really become *sākṣī*, like uranium becoming lead by transmutation. Then you won't get back the uranium. Then the possibility of the witness resolving in *Brahman*, that is, the possibility of liberation, would be absent. Light appears to undergo transformation but it never does. Suppose you focus light on a film. You see figures on the screen. The hero as well as the villain appear in the light. Do they contaminate the light or alter it? No. Similarly *caitanya*, as though, acquires the status of a *sākṣī*. Everything happens in *caitanya*. Nothing ever contaminates the *caitanya*.

Now this *sākṣī* descends into the intellect (*buddhi*), which is the seat of *rāgas*, *dveṣas* and sense of doership (*kartṛtva*) and enjoyership (*bhoktṛtva*). Now the *sākṣī* becomes the enjoyer and doer. When the person gets out of sleep, does he remain as the witness of the waking state? No. He suddenly becomes the *bhoktā*. He wants to have a cup of tea and read a newspaper. If you want to enjoy you have to work for it. Sense of enjoyment and doership go together. It is the folly of the Sāṅkhyas to separate *kartṛtva* from *bhokṛtva*. Thus, the *sākṣī* has already become the person.

The person goes out into the world through one or more sense-organs for enjoyment. He enjoys forms with the eyes, sounds with the ears, etc. If the forms and sounds remain outside, there is no enjoyment. They enter the mind through the sense-organs. Here the direction of this journey is reversed. The mind immediately projects likes and dislikes, depending upon whether the experience is pleasant or unpleasant. *Sukha*s and *duḥkha*s occur in the mind. Every *sukha* and *duḥkha* in its turn creates new *rāga*s and *dveṣa*s. Thus the false personality is further reinforced. This *bhramaṇa* goes on and on. The basis for this cycle is ignorance.

We are in the thralldom of time and space, *rāga* and *dveṣa*. There is no rational explanation for this. It is something that we experience day after day, life after life. It is illogical all right, but it is there in our life. A*jñāna* or illusion is not *pramāṇa siddha*, but it is *anubhava siddha*. That is why we use the word *Māyā*. This *saṁsāra* is not a product of rationale and logic. It is not established by a proper means of knowledge. But it is there by experience. It is the experience that establishes *ajñāna*. This is what is called *Māyā*. *Māyā* is neither a theory nor an explanation. It is just a statement of fact.

We need all the grace of *Īśvara* to overcome *Māyā*. At the level of *karmendriyas*, grace of *Īśvara* means that those *indriya*s are engaged in the actions of *dharma*. At the level of mind, grace signifies that all the emotions are directed towards *Īśvara*. For example, I would love to see beautiful things with the eyes. So, I visit the shrine of Lord Śrī Kṛṣṇa and enjoy the beautiful form of the Lord. I hear such a music that would help my mind to get absorbed in *Īśvara*. Thus, the basic tendency of the mind to enjoy things is now directed towards *Īśvara*. This is what is called *Īśvara* descending into the mind. Then, I use the intellect to know higher things of life like *ātman*. I discover the value of listening to *śāstra* (*śravaṇa*). The *buddhi* discovers value for *śravaṇa*. This is the grace of *Īśvara* at the level of *buddhi*.

We have to mainly address the problem of ego (*aham*). There is no fixed entity called *aham*. At one time, it is identified with the physical body. So we have: I am tall, I am short, etc. I am happy, I am unhappy: this is *aham* identifying with the mind. I am an attorney, I am a lawyer, I am a doctor: this is the identification of *aham* with the intellect. Another serious problem about this ego is that it is taken as enjoyer (*bhoktā*). Thus, the human being is permanently engaged in collecting and manipulating things, so as to enjoy them. Thus, the entire *saṁsāra* is centered around this *aham*. This *aham*, the sense of 'I', is the product of ignorance. I consider myself to be this small 'I'. This is the fundamental mistake committed by a human being. Since this small 'I' is known to me, it is an object parading as the subject. This is *Māyā*.

This small 'I' must be taken care of. It is the ego which denies the truth to us. We need not do anything with respect to the Supreme Reality. It is non-dual, self-evident and whole. It does not require any manipulation from our side. It is in the background of life all the time. We have to work for the elimination of this small 'I'. It is bound to disappear if we make effort in that direction. In the fight between truth and falsehood, the former is bound to win, since falsehood cannot stand in the presence of truth. We light a candle not to preserve it, but to consume the wax and the wick. Similarly, the *sādhanā* in the form of *upāsanā* by the *jijñāsu* helps to consume the ego, leaving the *ātman* in all its glory.

Some people use *upāsanā* for gaining transient benefits like heaven, or some results in this world like promotion in the job, or winning a court case, etc. There is nothing wrong in it, since *śāstra* itself offers us many such desire-based *karma*s and *upāsanā*s. But, any such *upāsanā* only reinforces the ego, thereby defeating the primary goal, namely *mokṣa*. One may ask: what is the advantage of knowing the truth about *ātman*? Truth is its own reward. By knowing truth, ignorance is cast away. That is good enough as a reward. The attitude of looking for a reward from outside oneself is a mistake resulting out of the ignorance of *ātman*, since *ātman* is *pūrṇa*. It is the habit of the enjoyer-ego to look for rewards. Knowledge of *ātman* does not bring in any special reward, but it includes all imaginable rewards and much more beyond that.

Ninth Verse

SURĒŚVARĀCĀRYA introduces the ninth verse of the *Dakṣiṇāmūrti Stotram* with a precise verse as follows:

> कथमेवंविधा माया निवर्तेतेति पृच्छतः ।
> ईश्वरोपासनारूपस्तदुपायः प्रकीर्त्यते ।।
> — *मानसोल्लासम्*, ९-१
>
> *kathamevaṁvidhā māyā nivarteteti pṛcchataḥ* ।
> *īśvaropāsanārūpastadupāyaḥ prakīrtyate* ।।
> — *Mānasollāsam*, 9-1
>
> Somebody may ask the question: How can this kind of *Māyā* be cast off ? The way to do that is to meditate upon *Īśvara*. This is explained in the ninth verse of the *Dakṣiṇāmūrti Stotram*.

Māyā was described in the earlier verses in some detail. It is shown that all our understanding of ourselves and of the world is an illusion. It was mentioned that time and space are mental categories. But we are at a loss as to how to come out of these mental categories? We are living in the prison of *saṁsāra*. Can we come out of that prison by the strength of our own effort? No. When a person falls into deep waters, he will nicely float till help arrives, if he maintains his balance of mind without getting frightened and stops struggling, because the specific gravity of the physical body is less than that of water. He need not do anything to save himself except to use the natural advantage of the difference in specific gravities of the body and the water. But if he struggles to keep afloat, he will surely drown. Similarly, a person who is imprisoned cannot come out of the prison simply on his own effort. But, if he follows the instruction from an outsider, he could successfully come out of the prison. In the same way, we need the help of *śāstra* and of *ācārya*, to cast away this *Māyā*. To gain the knowledge from the *śāstra* with the help of the teacher, and to own up that knowledge, we need the grace of *Īśvara* in abundance. Here comes the role of *upāsanā*. To know the reality, which is *Brahman*, we have to neutralise *ahaṅkāra* through an *upāsanā*. Worship of or meditation upon *Īśvara* requires an altar of *Īśvara*. This verse presents us with an altar which is closest to and the best representative of the Supreme Reality, the *Brahman*.

भूरंभास्यनलोनिलोंबरमहर्नाथो हिमांशुः पुमान्
इत्याभाति चराचरात्मकमिदं यस्यैव मूर्त्यष्टकम् ।
नान्यत्किंचन विद्यते विमृशतां यस्मात्परस्माद्विभोः
तस्मै श्रीगुरुमूर्तये नम इदं श्रीदक्षिणामूर्तये ।। ९।।

bhūraṁbhāsyanalonilomṁbaramaharnātho himāṁśuḥ pumān
ityābhāti carācarātmakamidaṁ yasyaiva mūrty-aṣṭakam ।
nānyatkiñcana vidyate vimṛśatāṁ yasmātparas-mādvibhoḥ
tasmai śrīgurumūrtaye nama idaṁ śrīdakṣiṇā-mūrtaye ।। 9 ।।

भूः (*bhūḥ*) — Earth, अंभांसी (*ambhāṁsī*) — waters, अनलहः (*analaḥ*) — fire, अनिलः (*anilaḥ*) — wind, अम्बरम् (*ambaram*) — space, अहर्नाथः (*aharnāthaḥ*) — Sun, हिमांशुः (*himāṁśuḥ*) — moon, पुमान् (*pumān*) — person, इति (*iti*) — thus, चराचरात्मकं (*carācarātmakam*) — consisting of moving and unmoving, इदम् (*idam*) — this universe,

यस्य (*yasya*) — of whom, मूर्त्यष्टकम् इव (*mūrtyaṣṭakam eva*) — eight-fold form alone, आभाति (*ābhāti*) — shining, विमृशतां (*vimṛśatāṁ*) — to those who have discrimination, परस्मात् (*parasmāt*) — Supreme, विभोः (*vibhoḥ*) — all-pervading, यस्मात् (*yasmāt*) — besides whom, अन्यत् (*anyat*) — other, किंचन (*kiñcana*) — whatever, न विद्यते (*na vidyate*) — does not exist, तस्मै श्रीगुरुमूर्तये नम इदं श्रीदक्षिणामूर्तये (*tasmai śrīgurumūrtaye nama idaṁ śrīdakṣiṇāmūrtaye*).

This universe, consisting of both the moving and the non-moving, is indeed shining as none other than the manifestation of the Lord in eight forms, namely, earth, waters, fire, wind, space, the sun, the moon and the person. In the vision of those who have a discerning faculty, there is nothing other than the Supreme Lord, who is all-pervading. That Lord is in the form of an incarnation of the teacher, Śrī Dakṣiṇāmūrti. My prostrations unto him.

Ātman is ever present as the substratum of everything. It is the ever-shining whole. There is nothing to be done by the seeker with reference to the eternal *ātman*. But, there is lot to be done on his part to dispel the ignorance which denies his own *svarūpa* to him. The seeker has to prepare himself as an instrument fit for this knowledge. He has to clean up his mind. We need not do anything about the Sun; it is enough if we open the window, when the Sun will flood the room with light. We have to demolish the walls of ignorance so painstakingly erected by ourselves. We have to get rid of a lot of dross in life, and make it easy for the mind to be free for the higher purpose. In life, we should apply an acid test before we hold onto something. The test is: do I need it? If the answer is 'no', then don't take it. If the answer is an emphatic yes, then take it and enjoy it by all means. For example, do I need to attend a particular party? If no, don't go. What shall I do at home? You need not do any thing. First, you stop going. Whether you go instead to a Vedānta class or not, first stop going to the party, because you don't need it. This is what is called *upāsanā* in life.

You live in the time-space framework and to gain the Truth you have to transcend that framework. What instrument do you have to transcend the time-space framework? The mind alone. But can it function outside the time-space framework? No. You have to overcome the mind with the help of the mind. *Paramātman* has to be seen with the help of the mind. But the moment you see *Īśvara* there will be no mind. This is the essence of *Māyā*.

As long as your mind is engrossed in the things of the world and it is filled with jealousy, envy, anger, anxiety, etc., you can't realise the Supreme Reality. Unless you realise the Supreme Reality you can't come out of the bondage of *saṁsāra*. What a dilemma! Only the grace of *Īśvara* can save us. In fact, the grace is already in you. You have a heart which desires this truth. You have a body and a life-force, which help you to make an effort in that direction. All of this is given to you. None of it is your creation. The Power, which has given you all this, will also make you see the truth.

In Yoga there is only victory, no defeat. Yoga means knowledge and also the effort to gain that knowledge. It is a fight between truth and untruth. No seeker would lose this fight, because untruth can never stand before truth.

सत्यमेव जयते नानृतम् । — *मुण्डकोपनिषद्*, ३-१-६

satyameva jayate nānṛtam । — *Muṇḍakopaniṣad*, 3-1-6

Truth (truthful person) alone triumphs; not untruth.

It is better to go through all stages of life before you really plunge into *ātma-jñāna*. It is like entering into a palace by climbing up the steps. Hanumān can jump all the steps at a stroke and make it too. But you may not be able to do that. So there is *upāsanā* at all levels. There is an *upāsanā* for a student to get a higher rank; there is an *upāsanā* for a businessman for gaining profit. A mother can perform *upāsanā* for the advancement of her children in life. All these *upāsanā*s are within the parameters of *saṁsāra*. They won't take you out of *saṁsāra*.

As long as the candle struggles to preserve the wick and wax, it cannot give light to others. Similarly if you want to gain *ātma-jñāna,* you can't retain the small person. Some people want to retain their gender also when they go to the other *loka*s. You can understand how deeply the gender has affected their psyche. The fact is that the gender stops at the level of the body. The sense-organs, mind, intellect, ego and the awareness in which all these shine are not gender-specific. If you want to retain your personality in terms of gender or *rāga* and *dveṣa* you can't have light. It is like a candle that remains as it is without giving light even after several years because it refuses to sacrifice its wick and wax. You should work hard to make life simple in terms of attachments, likes and dislikes. You should divest yourself from all this trash. You should make yourself a fit instrument for the truth. There comes the role of *upāsanā*.

So you need to do *upāsanā* to gain the grace of *Īśvara*. The purpose of *upāsanā* here is not to manipulate the *saṁsāra*. As long as you struggle to establish yourself in the *saṁsāra*, you are denying the truth to yourself. People armour themselves against the truth and knowledge. Then where from the knowledge will come?

Upāsanā: *upa* means near; *āsana* is 'staying put'. We

stick with *Īśvara*, which is the only Truth. There is no difficulty in this *upāsanā*. People have a wrong notion that it is very difficult for them to understand *upāsanā*. In fact, it is relatively easier than *saṁsāra*. For an *upāsaka*, life becomes a blessing to himself as well as to people around him. In the family he is the least demanding and the most accommodating person. Other members of the family would love him. A demanding person is a problem for everybody in the family, though they may not complain for fear of consequences. An *upāsaka* is likewise an asset to the society around him. He is loved and respected all around. Like a monkey holds onto the higher branch while leaving the lower one, the seeker holds on to his pursuit of knowledge, as the hold on *saṁsāra* gradually slackens.

Upāsanā is of two kinds: one is limited to a given altar, a fixed place and time. We all worship the Lord in an idol at an altar in the house and also in the temple. We have fixed timings for this, like morning before sunrise or evening after sunset. We reserve some special days for visiting the Lord in the temple. The other kind of *upāsanā* surpasses all these limitations and hence it is superior to the former. Dakṣiṇāmūrti *upāsanā* is of the superior kind. In it there is no possibility of the seeker being away from the altar at any time. Whether I reflect upon it or not, the altar of the Lord is always before me. *Parameśvara* is not sitting somewhere above. He is not external to the world. He is the *antaryāmin*. He is the reality of this whole world. He is the fragrance of the flowers, the brilliance of the Sun, and the coolness and beauty of the moon. He is the glory of the river Gaṅgā, and of the rains. He is the sweltering heat of the summer. He is the bright shining yellow colour of the gold. He is the black strength of the steel. He is the hardness of the diamond. He is the toughness of the fibre. He is every thing. He is the destructive power of the uranium atom. He is the curing property of the medicinal herbs. He is the intrinsic property, called *dharma*, of every object in this universe. He is the *ātman* of everything. The entire universe exists in *Īśvara*.

Mūrti is a very popular word used for naming a person. In Andhra Pradesh, we come across many *mūrti*s; *Satyanārāyaṇamūrti*, *Kṛṣṇamūrti*, etc., *Mūrti* means a form. *Viṣṇumūrti* means a manifestation or a specific form of Viṣṇu. Every *jīva* is essentially a form (*mūrti*) of *Īśvara* alone. *Jīivatva* is a relative status brought onto the infinite consciousness by ignorance. Essentially the awareness shining in the heart of a living being is *Īśvara* alone.

ईश्वरस्सर्वभूतानां हृद्देशेऽर्जुन तिष्ठति ।

— *श्रीमद्भगवद्गीता*, १८-६१

īśvarassarvabhūtānāṁ hṛddeśer'juna tiṣṭhati ।

— *Śrīmadbhagavad-Gītā*, 18-61

O Arjuna, *Īśvara* abides in the hearts of all living beings.

Therefore every human being can be named after the Lord. We may name one Viṣṇu, another Śiva. This verse prescribes eight specific *mūrti*s (*aṣṭamūrti*s) of *Īśvara* for the purpose of worship and meditation of *Īśvara* in one or more forms.

What are these *aṣṭamūrti*s? By the time these eight *mūrti*s of *Īśvara* are understood by us, our whole concept of *Īśvara* would change. In Vedānta we say that there is *Īśvara* (*īśvaraḥ asti*). In that we are on the side of the theologians standing opposite to the materialists (*nāstika*s), or agnostics. Our similarity with theologians however ends there. When we say *īśvaraḥ asti*, we don't mean it the same way as theologians. Their *Īśvara* is a big and powerful entity sitting somewhere above and outside the universe (*parokṣa*). But our *Īśvara* is now and here (*pratyakṣa*). Some people have a mindset commited to the *parokṣa*. On the other hand, in Vedānta we say that *Īśvara* is in the form of the universe before us. *Īśvara* pervades this entire universe, and hence is called Viṣṇu. But for the purpose of easily relating to *Īśvara*, this verse points out eight *vibhūti*s (glories crystallised) of *Īśvara*. These *vibhūti*s are the *aṣṭamūrti*s.

Bhūḥ means earth. Earth is *Īśvara*. That means, we are literally standing upon *Īśvara*. It is not the physical earth alone. The entire living system along with ecology and environment is called *Bhūḥ*. In the *Gītā*, Bhagavān says:

गामाविश्य च भूतानि धारयाम्यहमोजसा । (१५-१३)
gāmāviśya ca bhūtāni dhārayāmyahamojasā । (15-13)

I possess the earth and uphold the life and other things with my strength.

The capacity to withstand intense pressure or super-heavy weight is called *ojaḥ*. Earth sustains both the living and the non-living beings. The core of the earth is very hot but on the surface it is mostly pleasant and hospitable. When we get up from the bed in the morning, we recite a verse of prayer to the earth, before keeping the feet on it, which is unavoidable.

समुद्रवसने देवि पर्वतस्तनमंडले ।
विष्णुपत्नि नमस्तुभ्यं पादस्पर्शं क्षमस्व मे ।।

samudravasane devi parvatastanamaṇḍale ।
viṣṇupatni namastubhyaṁ pādasparśaṁ kṣamasva me ।।

O Goddess! the ocean is your garment and the mountain ranges are your bosom. You are the consort of Lord Viṣṇu. Forgive me for touching you with the feet. My prostrations unto you.

This prayer reflects the attitude of humility on the part of the seeker and it is conducive to the cultivation of devotion. The moment the seeker gets out of the bed, his *upāsanā* is on. He need not wait for bath or run to a temple. All the temples are around him. This *upāsanā* does not come in the way of other chores of life. On the other hand, the regular work would be blessed by this *upāsanā*. Suppose you go for a walk. That time can be very profitably utilised for this *upāsanā*, which will help the seeker in the long run to transcend the mind. *Upāsanā* doesn't mean just meditation for half an hour in the morning and half an hour in the evening. It is a lifestyle.

Aṁbhāṁsi means waters. Of course, water is an incarnation of *Īśvara*. We can look at water from two standpoints. Water is a compound of hydrogen and oxygen atoms. This information together with various other physical and chemical properties is called knowledge. But Bhagavān says something more about water in the *Gītā:*

रसोऽहमप्सु कौंतेय । (७-८)
raso'hamapsu kaunteya । (7-8)

O Arjuna, I am the taste in the waters.

Water is life. In Sanskrit, *jīvana* means water. It also means life. This is wisdom. This is the reason why we worship every river. Delaware river near our *aśrama* in the U.S. is as sacred to me as Gaṅgā. River is a life-sustaining system. Many civilizations have grown on the banks of the rivers. In *kumbhābhiṣeka*, *Īśvara* is anointed with water, which is also *Īśvara*. All over India *Īśvara* is worshipped in the form of a *liṅga*. Most of them are made with stone or some such related material (*pārthiva liṅgam*). If we want to worship *Īśvara* in the form of *liṅga*, we can just make a *liṅga* with wet clay and use it as an altar. Similarly, water also can serve as the altar. We have water-*liṅga* in Jambūkeśvar, Tamil Nadu.

Anala is fire. Fire is the universal altar in the Vedic culture. The very first *mantra* of the *Ṛgveda* starts with the praise of the *Īśvara* in the form of *agni*.

> अग्निमीडे पुरोहितं यज्ञस्य देवमृत्विजम् ।
> *agnimīḍe purohitaṁ yajñasya devamṛtvijam* ।
>
> I praise the glory of agni, who is the Lord of the Vedic ritual in the form of the Vedic priest and who is the foremost benefactor.

Agni is the altar for offering the oblations of ghee, etc., to different *devatā*s. The entire ritualistic portion of the Veda (*karma-kāṇḍa*) is dependent on Agni. Agni pervades the entire universe. When we strike a match stick, the all-pervading fire manifests as a small flame. When we put off a lamp, the small flame of the lamp merges into the great element, fire. The smallness of the fire is with respect to *upādhi*, the medium through which it manifests. The *Pañcadaśī* describes the relative volumes of these elements in the universe. Waters are ten times Pṛthvī, the solid stuff of the universe. Even on earth, water occupies double the area of land mass. Agni is ten times more than waters. Vāyu pervades ten times more than Agni.

The ever-burning solar orb is Agni. The digestive fire in the stomach is another manifestation of that *mahāgni*. Bhagavān refers to this digestive fire as himself in the *Gītā*:

> अहं वैश्वानरो भूत्वा प्राणिनां देहमाश्रितः ।
> प्राणापानसमायुक्तः पचाम्यन्नं चतुर्विधम् ।। (१५-१४)
>
> *aham vaiśvānaro bhūtvā prāṇinām dehamāśritaḥ* ।
> *prāṇāpānasamāyuktaḥ pacāmyannaṁ caturvidham* ।।
> (15-14)

Having become the digestive fire obtaining in the bodies of living beings, endowed with *prāṇa* and *apāna*, I cook the four-fold food.

Anilaḥ: *nilaya* means a fixed place of dwelling. Vāyu has no such *nilaya*; hence the name *anilaḥ* (*na nilayati*). He is everywhere. He roams all over. The wind is another very important altar of *Īśvara*. In *prāṇāyāma,* it is at this altar that a seeker worships. *Prāṇāyāma* is a useful technique for clearing the mind of its restlessness; it should be practised as such. But, if it is exaggerated to such an extent to claim that it gives liberation, then that is wrong. *Prāṇa* becomes a means to attain *Īśvara*, because *prāṇa* is the manifestation of *Īśvara*. *Prāṇa* is not limited to your body. Suppose I look at myself as a bundle of blood, heart, spleen, liver, eyes, ears, nose, etc., then the notion that I am a limited being becomes very strong. On the other hand, if I look at myself as the *prāṇa,* it helps me to overcome this calamitous body-identity. I am the life-force that pervades the body. When we do *prāṇāyāma,* we shift the attention from the body to the life-force which pervades the body. That is *prāṇāyāma*. When the focus of the mind is thus shifted from the body to the *prāṇa*, the truth that I am literally living in the lap of *Īśvara* in the form of all-pervading *prāṇa* becomes obvious.

नमस्ते वायो । त्वमेव प्रत्यक्षं ब्रह्मासि ।

— *तैत्तिरीयोपनिषत्*, १-१

namaste vāyo । *tvameva pratayakṣaṁ brahmāsi* ।

— *Taittirīyopaniṣad*, 1-1

O Vāyu, my salutations unto you. You are indeed the *Brahman* available for direct perception.

Prāṇāyāma helps us to realise this vision. If we practise *prāṇāyāma* with this understanding for a length of time, the false notion of identifying with the body is diluted.

Ākāśa: It is more pervading than all other great elements. The other four exist in *Ākāśa. Ākāśa* is the closest to *Īśvara* in many respects. The *Taittirīyopaniṣad* describes the *Brahman* as the one with space as body.

आकाशशरीरं ब्रह्म । (१-१४)

ākāśaśarīraṁ brahma । (1-14)

The *Brahman* has space as its body.

There is a *ākāśa-liṅga* in Chidambaram of Tamil Nadu. The priests worship the space, which is *Īśvara*. That is the secret of Chidambaram (*cidaṁbara rahasya*).

There is a school of thought which holds *ākāśa* as void. This is wrong. *Ākāśa* is as much physical (material) as the other four elements. Modern physics recognised space as physical by coining the term 'curved space'. The space around the Sun is more curved due to higher gravitational force than that around us, the earth. We are saying pretty much the same thing since ages that space is material in nature; but it is very subtle; so subtle that you can't make parts out of it. It is *niravayava.*

These five elements are more and more subtle in the order discussed above. The physical body is made up of these five elements alone. In fact, there is a general law in Vedānta. Whatever is found in the universe (*brahmāṇḍa*) is also found in the physical body of the human being (*piṇḍāṇḍa*).

The sixth form of the Lord is the Sun, the Lord of the day-light (*aharnāthaḥ*). Once again Bhagavān presents himself as the Sun bearing the name Viṣṇu.

आदित्यानामहं विष्णुर्ज्योतिषां रविरंशुमान् । (१०-२१)

ādityānāmahaṁ viṣṇurjyotiṣāṁ raviraṁśumān । (10-21)

Among the Ādityas I am Viṣṇu; among the luminaries, the Sun, the one who has many rays.

So the Sun in the sky is a marvellous manifestation of the Lord. He is called Sūrya Nārāyaṇa, the Lord in the form of the Sun. But, people take *Īśvara* as *parokṣa* (out of sight), while he is brilliantly shining all the time before our very eyes. There was an unfortunate child who lost his mother. The child asked: where is the mother? The father answered: the mother is in the heaven. That gives some solace to the child, and makes it easier for the child to cope with its life. People who are sure that the Lord is in heaven are spiritual babies. They feel some comfort in the idea of a non-local God. The famous *Gāyatrī mantra* is a *mahāvākya*, that is, a profound statement which teaches the identity of *jīva* and *Īśvara* in the form of the Sun.

The Moon is the seventh form of the Lord with eight forms. Once again, Lord Śrī Kṛṣṇa introduces himself as the moon.

नक्षत्राणामहं शशी । (१०-२१)

nakṣatrāṇāmahaṁ śaśī । (10-21)

I am the Moon, the Lord of stars.

As usual, the Sun and the moon are present not only in the world but also in the body. The vital air of the body, *prāṇa* is the Sun and *apāna* is the moon.

Finally, the eighth altar is yourself, *pumān*. Whosoever excludes himself from this universe which is *Īśvara*, has a problem, just like Arjuna. If you include yourself in the universe, the problem of *saṁsāra* disappears at once. A person who isolates himself while travelling in a group faces difficulties. A deer in a herd is safe. If it comes out of the herd, it is no more safe. The human being is like a wave in the ocean. Once the person isolates himself, in his understanding, from the universe, he becomes one against everything else. The person is essentially *ātman*, which is none other than *Īśvara*. All said and done, there is no *Īśvara* outside *ātman*. If *Īśvara* were to be different from *ātman*, that is *anātman*, then He becomes insentient (*jaḍa*), the seen (*dṛśya*), subject to modification (*vikārī*) and subject to destruction (*vināśī*).

Viśvarūpa upāsanā and *aṣṭamūrti upāsanā* are very fundamental to Vedānta. There are four varieties of devotees: *ārta*, the one in distress; *arthārthī*, the aspiring one; *jijñāsu*, the one desirous of the knowledge of *ātman* and *jñānī*, the wise one. *Ārta bhakta* is the one who is trying to come out of difficulties with the help of *Īśvara*. *Arthārthī bhakta* is the one who tries to gain something in life, some elevation in career, etc., with the help of *Īśvara*. In these two types of *bhakti*s, the devotee is fundamentally a limited being. He is not keen to enquire into his limitations. He takes himself to be a limited being and approaches *Īśvara* for a worldly purpose. In his approach to *Īśvara*, he is basically guided by fear in one case, and desire in the other case. Such a devotee normally worships *Īśvara* in a given form suitable to his psychology.

Human being has two fundamental emotions, namely, desire and fear. A person is constantly out to gain something or to avoid something else. He continuously seeks pleasure and tries to keep pain away. This pursuit of pleasure is the fundamental cause of the misery. Pain visits us without our seeking it. Similarly, pleasure would also come to us on its own. Why should we seek pleasure and become miserable in the process? Whatever good happened in one's life was due to the grace of *Īśvara*. The moment a person matures to an extent where he stops seeking pleasure, he becomes eligible for the knowledge of *ātman*. But, overcoming desire and fear is not easy. So we need help for that. When I can't do a thing on my own, the intelligent way out is to seek help. Suppose my vehicle broke down somewhere on the road, then I should seek somebody's help, without being self-conscious. Therefore, a *jijñāsu* is advised to worship *Īśvara* to earn the grace for overcoming the thraldom of *saṁsāra*. *Viśvarūpa* or *aṣṭamūrti upāsanā* is best suited for a *jijñāsu bhakta* to loosen the bonds of desire and fear and cast them aside.

We play many roles in life. The correct way of playing a role is to do the duty dictated by the role with a sense of detachment, without investing a lot of emotion into that role. We err in making big emotional investments into the roles played by us. These human relationships are really funny. As long as a particular relationship is going on, it appears to be nice and firm. But a small aberration disturbs it and the entire edifice of the relationship comes crashing down. Attachment born of ignorance is a very weak and unreliable foundation. We do need an *upāsanā* to overcome the attachment to the things of the world. I am not suggesting that we should turn our heart into a stone. We should have all the love and compassion in the world. But, we should strive to expand the boundaries of this love further and further, such that one day we will be able to love not only the entire humanity but also all the living beings.

You have two bodies, one a personal body, and the other a universal body. Both bodies are made up of the same set of five elements. Both bodies are recognised in the same way, with the help of the five sense-organs and mind. But, we are identified with the personal body so much that we are totally ignorant of the universal body. *Viśvarūpa upāsanā* corrects this situation. Identity is the Truth; division is false. This is the bottom line of Vedāntic vision. That does not mean that I will lose my body. The body is there with me, not because of my loving or attachment to it; but because of the natural order and *prārabdha*. This expansion of the vision does not make me lose the few things that I have. I continue to be in their possession. The only difference is that I recognise that I do not own them. The wrong notions of me and mine will be diluted by this *upāsanā*.

Viśvarūpa upāsanā purifies the mind and slowly consumes the small person, who is essentially made up of an *ahaṅkāra, kartṛtva, bhoktṛtva*, and a set of likes and dislikes, etc. To know the truth, we should cross the limitations imposed by the mind. We will be able to cross the mind only if it is pure. We cannot leave behind the impurities of likes and dislikes in the mind and expect to transcend it. Suppose you have a knee pain. As long as that pain persists, you are stuck with your knee. The moment that pain goes away, you don't even remember your knee. Similarly as long as there are strong likes and dislikes in the mind, you can never cross the confines of the mind; and to that extent, you are away from the truth. You continue to live in your own world, which has nothing to do with the truth.

There are apparently two contradictory statements in Upaniṣads:

यतो वाचो निवर्तंते । अप्राप्य मनसा सह ।
— *तैत्तिरीयोपनिषद्*, २-९-१

yato vāco nivartante । *aprāpya manasā saha* ।
— *Taittirīyopaniṣad*, 2-9-1

The words together with the mind returned, having failed to attain *Brahman*.

मनसैवानुद्रष्टव्यम् । — *कठोपनिषद्*, २-१-११
manasaivānudraṣṭavyam । — *Kaṭhopaniṣad*, 2-1-11

This *Brahman* has to be attained with the mind alone.

The purport of the first statement is that an impure mind cannot attain *Brahman*, which is *ātman*. The second statement clarifies that the purified mind alone can help us attain the *ātman* by resolving in it. This purification is readily achieved by *viśvarūpa upāsanā*. This *upāsanā* is a wonderful *sāttvika* activity aimed at complete elimination of *tamo-guṇa* (inertia or laziness to think and delusion) of the mind. People are lazy to think. Suppose I teach the story of the *Rāmāyaṇa* or the *Bhāgavata*. I would attract a large crowd. If I teach the *Dakṣiṇāmūrti Stotram*, I will only have select people as audience.

And then the mind can be hyperactive (*rajo-guṇa*) too. It is often very agitated. There is always, as it were, a big traffic jam of thoughts in the mind. One cannot have a meaningul life with a hyperactive mind; leave alone understanding the higher truths of life. You have to take care of your mind first. Disease starts in the mind and then settles into the body.

A single word or a statement will help you to reach the truth, provided your mind is ready for it. Suppose you are looking for a person everywhere, while that person has always been in your presence. In such a situation, a brief and precise statement by a friend is enough for you to gain what you are seeking. The knowing of *ātman* is excactly similar to that. But if the mind is clean and appropriate effort is put in, the *mahāvākya* or the teaching will help you to see the truth very clearly. Therefore when the *upāsanā* is in place, it is very helpful.

Nānyatkiñcana vidyate vimr̥śatāṁ yasmāt-parasmā-dvibhoḥ: The essence of *Visvarūpa upāsanā* can be summarised in one brief statement: *Dr̥śyamātre īśvarabuddhiḥ*. We have to develop an attitude of mind, which recognises the *tattva* (reality) without getting engrossed in just names and forms. Our mind normally functions that way. When we go to a jewellery shop, we straightaway get engrossed with various ornaments, and fail to recognise the unity of all of them in the gold. Our minds are very much enchanted and attracted by whatever appears on the surface. We should learn to see in and through *nāma-rūpa* and go for *tattva. Tattva* is defined as *anāropita ākāra.* Truth is gained by rejecting the superimposition of form. As long as we are very busy in observing the shape and form, we will never be able to know the *tattva.*

We should reduce, in our vision, the entire world of plurality to its *tattva* in which all forms appear. As a first step, the entire universe can be reduced to the five great elements. Though earth, moon, etc., have characteristic shapes, Pr̥thvī as an element has no particular form. Water also has no particular form. But it acquires the form of the vessel in which it is contained. These five elements are nothing but superimpositions on *Īśvara.* So whatever we are looking at is *Īśvara.* So God is very much before us in the form of *jagat.*

The universe is nothing but Matter. The table is Matter. The pot is Matter. Air around us is Matter. Water in the rivers and the oceans is also Matter. Fire (dense collection of hot gases radiating light and heat) is Matter. We have seen that space is also Matter. There is one Matter, which is manifest as five great elements. Every object in this universe is made up of the combination of only those five elements. Thus the *masala* or *dhātu* of all the objects of this universe is Matter. That Matter is non-dual; there is nothing other than that. That Matter, that *vastu,* is called *Brahman.* That *Brahman* is *caitanya* and that *caitanya* is you.

Vimr̥śatām: For the seekers who are ready to see through the *nāma-rūpa*, and see more than what eyes can show . . .

for such people, all this plurality is just an appearance, like the plurality on the cinema screen. The only truth about the movie is the light in which the entire movie appears. Similarly the entire universe appears in *Brahman*. So the web and weft of this universe is *Brahman*.

Therefore a person, who is earnest to know the truth, who has a high value for the truth, who is ready to invest the life for gaining the truth, who is ready to pay the price of the finite to gain the Infinite, and who has prepared himself with the help of this *upāsanā*, will gain this knowledge now and here. He is liberated from the bondage of *saṁsāra*, even while leading an active life.

Tenth Verse

It is customary in the *stotra* literature to allot at the end at least one verse to say some encouraging words about the results that would accrue to the seeker by reciting, understanding and assimilating the said *stotra*. Śrī Śaṅkara concludes this *stotra* also with one such verse of *phalaśruti*, which again excels many verses of that kind in the sense that the result mentioned is in accordance with the teaching presented in the entire *stotra*.

सर्वात्मत्वमिति स्फुटीकृतमिदं यस्मादमुष्मिंस्तवे
तेनास्य श्रवणात्तदर्थमननाद्ध्यानाच्च संकीर्तनात् ।
सर्वात्मत्वमहाविभूतिसहितं स्यादीश्वरत्वं स्वतः
सिद्ध्येत्तत्पुनरष्टधा परिणतं चैश्वर्यमव्याहतम् ।। १० ।।

sarvātmatvamiti sphuṭīkṛtamidaṁ yasmādamuṣmiṁstave
tenāsya śravaṇāttadarthamananāddhyānācca saṅkīrtanāt ।
sarvātmatvamahāvibhūtisahitaṁ syādīśvaratvaṁ svataḥ
siddhyettatpunaraṣṭadhā pariṇatañcaiśvaryama vyāhatam ।।

यस्मात् (*yasmāt*) — because, इति (*iti*) — thus, अमुष्मिन् (*amuṣmin*) — in this, स्तवे (*stave*) — encomium, इदम् (*idam*) — this, सर्वात्मत्वम् (*sarvātmatvam*) — being all,

स्फुटीकृतम् (*sphuṭīkṛtam*) — vividly described, तेना (*tenā*) — for that reason, अस्य (*asya*) — of this, श्रवणात् (*śravaṇāt*) — by listening to, तदर्थमननात् (*tadarthamananāt*) — by investigating its meaning, ध्यानात् (*dhyānāt*) — by contemplation, च (*ca*) — and, संकीर्तनात् (*saṅkīrtanāt*) — by recitation, सर्वात्मत्वमहाविभूतिसहितं (*sarvātmatvamahā-vibhūtisahitaṁ*) — together with the great glory of being all, इश्वरत्वं (*īśvaratvaṁ*) — overlordship, स्वतः (*svataḥ*) — on its own, स्यात् (*syāt*) — comes, पुनः (*punaḥ*) — again, च (*ca*) — and, अष्टधा (*aṣṭadhā*) — in an eight-fold way, परिणतं (*pariṇataṁ*) — manifested, अव्याहतम् (*avyāhatam*) — without impediments, तत् (*tat*) — that, एश्वर्यम् (*aiśvaryam*) — the glory of psychic and mystic powers, सिद्ध्येत् (*siddhyet*) — gets accomplished.

In this encomium, the truth about *ātman* being all, is thus made very clear. Therefore, by listening to its exposition by the teacher, by ruminating on its meaning, by reflecting upon it and by reciting it, the seeker gains the eternal supreme glory of being the *Brahman* which is all. In addition to that, he gains the overlordship consisting of unassailable eight-fold power.

We have seen at length that the world appearing before us is none other than so many forms of the Lord. Also, we have an inner world of emotions, namely, a sense of agency of actions, and a sense of enjoyership, etc. Normally, we are quite knowledgeable about the goings-on outside, but we are ignorant of this inner world. As long as a person is ignorant of his own thought processes, he is a slave to them. He cannot do anything about them, as long as he is ignorant about them. Therefore, we have to take care of the inner world also. The entire process of personality development or maturity starts with the recognition of this fact.

People normally think that their problems have origins in the outside. For example, a gentleman thinks that he has problems at home because of the other members of the family; and also he has problems in the office because of his seniors as well as juniors. But, in the vision of the Vedānta, a person's problems are entirely the creation of his own mind. If this premise is accepted, then the *Gītā* or Vedānta can play a very useful role in mitigating those problems. As long as a person thinks that his problems lie outside, and tries to manipulate the world to suit his needs, that effort will not come to an end in this life or in a million lives that would follow. Therefore, we should recognise that the problem is within and hence, the solution is also within the person.

If one can carefully cultivate this inwardness (*antar-mukhatva*), then it will culminate in what is called *sarvātmatva* or *sarvātma bhāva*. That means, I am that *ātman* which includes the entire universe. This is the topic discussed at length at the beginning of *Dakṣiṇāmūrti Stotram*. *Viśvam nijāntargam*. Some effort is required to appreciate this vision.

I am a small speck of an object lying in a corner of the universe, and the entire universe of plurality is outside me. This is how the mind looks at things. All the theologies of the world do not help much to improve this hopeless situation. I am a limited being and facing me is an enormous and an overwhelming world. What chance do I have before it? In contrast, Vedānta places a challenging proposition before us. Are you ready for it? You are not just one more object in this universe. In fact, you are the subject with reference to the entire universe.

You are the knower who is aware of the galaxies, stars, the sun, planets, globe, mountains, rivers, humans, animals, birds, etc. The entire universe with its infinite objects stands opposite to you as an object of your awareness. You are not one more object. First, you remove yourself from the side of the world. Stand on the side of the awareness. That is where you belong. You are a conscious being (*sat-cit ātman*). You are the awareness, which illuminates the entire universe. You look in the eastern direction. You illumine the entire objects of the eastern direction; same with the other quarters also. You are the centre of this universe. Bhagavān describes in the *Gītā*, *kṣetrajña* as the knower of the field and the entire universe as the field. If you could elevate yourself from this false identification with the physical body, because of which you became one more object, then you realise that the life (*prāṇa*) of all living beings of this universe is not different from you. Everything has its existence in the awareness, and that awareness is you.

How is it that everything is in *caitanya*? Here is a pot. I see the pot. But what is seen by me is not the pot which is supposed to be outside; I see the pot in the form of pot-*vṛtti* of the mind. When I look at you in the photograph, I am not looking at you outside the photograph. When I am reading a book, I am reading the *mānasa pustaka*, the image of the book in the mind. Thus one part of the mind is the object and another part of the same mind is the subject. What is this mind? It is nothing but a motion in the infinite ocean of homogeneous (*ekarasa*), attributeless (*nirviśeṣa*) awareness. That awareness (*jñāna*) is the origin of all concepts of space and time, inside and outside. Therefore, it is the one seeing that becomes the seer and the seen. Both the seer and the seen arise from and set in that awareness simultaneously. You are that *caitanya*. It is like one wave rising in the ocean and enveloping another wave, while their essential content is the same water.

That is what is called *sarvātmatva*. This *sarvātmatva* is

explained by Śrī Śaṅkara in this *stotra*. What a marvellous *stotra* it is! The entire religious and spiritual life of a seeker culminates in the teaching of this *stotra*. One has to carefully listen to it from the teacher. Vedānta is not something which is read in paperbacks; it is something which is gained by listening to the exposition by the teacher. Paperbacks help to create interest and perhaps enthusiasm in Vedānta for the reader. There is an important reason for this. While reading, the egotism of the reader is intact, whereas while listening to in the presence of the revered teacher, it is kept in abeyance. Ego is the only obstacle for this knowledge. Also, one can not figure it out all by oneself. Therefore the *Bṛhadāraṇyaka śruti* says:

> आत्मा वा अरे द्रष्टव्यः श्रोतव्यः। (२-४-५)
> *ātmā vā are draṣṭavyaḥ śrotavyaḥ* । (2-4-5)
>
> O Maitreyī! One should know about *ātman* by listening to it.

Normally, at the end of the *stotra*s, it is mentioned that the seeker will gain the results by reciting the *stotra*. Not so in the case of this *stotra*; because, it is more a teaching than a simple eulogy. Hence, it is recommended for *śravaṇa*, followed by *manana*, namely, dwelling upon the same subject-matter further, till all the doubts about it are cleared.

People recite *stotra*s without even bothering to know the meaning. Even such a recitation gives some result. It has its own value. But, this *stotra* is not like any other *stotra*. This is teaching in a condensed form. But, it has all the qualities of a *stotra* and also gives many benefits by recitation. But, we have to contemplate on the meaning (*dhyānāt*), so that the teaching becomes our own. When the mind is agitated, just observe it as a witness; it calms down. You will gain that extra space. This is how we do contemplation (*nididhyāsana*).

You should live as a witness to your own life at least for sometime in the day. It requires a lot of sincerity, earnestness and enthusiasm.

Meditation in Vedānta consists of entering into subtler and subtler levels of consciousness by controlling the grosser levels. When the body is negated by understanding, you are one with the *prāṇa*. When the *prāṇa* is negated, you are one with the mind. This process continues. It may be mentioned in this context that *mantra jāpa* is a very useful exercise in preparing the mind for such contemplation.

A devotee was on his way to see *Īśvara*. Indra met him on the way and offered the devotee a seat in heaven. The devotee politely refused, saying that he was not interested in heaven. A little later Kubera appeared before him and offered treasures. Once again, the devotee was not interested. He continued on his path. Sometime later, he casually looked back, only to find Indra and Kubera earnestly following him. We may not be keen about the *phalaśruti*. Truth is its own reward. There cannot be greater benefit to knowledge than dispelling ignorance. You see a rope and understand it as a rope. That is good enough. Suppose you failed to recognise the rope as a rope. Immediately your mind projects a snake and you are in serious trouble. This knowledge deserves investment of effort of a lifetime.

Saṅkīrtana means teaching nicely to others. If a person is capable of teaching, and if a *jijñāsu* approaches him, then he is duty-bound to teach him. But, it should not be taught unless the seeker approaches the teacher. Śrī Śaṅkara has not kept the knowledge to himself. He composed *Dakṣiṇāmūrti Stotram*.

Siddhi means a psychic power. In Vedānta, such *siddhis*

are not held in high esteem. What we need is *mahāsiddhi*, and the *sarvātmatva* explained above is that *mahāsiddhi*. In addition to that, a few other benefits (*siddhi*s) also will accrue to the devotee automatically. Śrī Sureśvara explained these secondary results in a very interesting fashion.

> पाके प्रवर्तमानस्य शीतादिपरिहारवत् ।
> प्रासंगिकाश्च सिध्यंति स्तोत्रेणानेन सर्वदा ।।
> — *मानसोल्लासः*, १०-३
>
> *pāke pravartamānasya śītādiparihāravat* ।
> *prāsaṅgikāśca sidhyanti stotreṇānena sarvadā* ।।
> — *Mānasollāsaḥ*, 10-3
>
> A person who is cooking food is automatically relieved from cold. Similarly, this *stotra* brings in secondary benefits to the devotee all the time.
>
> पुष्पमानयता गंधो विनेच्छामनुभूयते ।
> पूर्णाहंभावयुक्तेन परिच्छिन्ना विभूतयः ।।
> — *मानसोल्लासः*, १०-६
>
> *puṣpamānayatā gandho vinecchāmanubhūyate* ।
> *pūrṇāhaṁbhāvayuktena paricchinnā vibhūtayaḥ* ।।
> — *Mānasollāsaḥ*,10-6
>
> A person carrying flowers enjoys their fragrance even without a desire for doing so. A person who understands that his essential nature (*ātman*) is the whole, enjoys some powers, which are limited in nature.

Knowledge of *ātman* bestows all other *siddhi*s on the devotee, because *ātman* includes the entire universe within itself.

Reciting these verses is a great virtue (*puṇya*) by itself. Recitation coupled with reflection brings in auspiciousness (*maṅgaḷa*) to you and keeps inauspicious things away, because it is *brahma-jñāna*. While taking care of the fundamental problem, the topical problem is also automatically solved without any special effort on the part of the devotee.

So, we should aim to know *Brahman*, without giving undue importance to petty things in life. We should have a broader vision. If one has to hunt, one should hunt a lion, not a rabbit. If you have to ask *Īśvara* for something, it should be *brahma-jñāna*. You should not seek some silly things. They will be yours anyway (*caiśvaryam avyāhatam*). *Ātma-jñāna* is the fulfilment of this human life. So, it is there very much in your destiny. As a human being, you are destined to know this truth. Only you have to yearn and work for it. You may have to sacrifice the finite for the sake of the Infinite. You richly deserve it. I don't have even an iota of doubt that you are all *Brahman*.

ओं पूर्णमदः पूर्णमिदं पूर्णात्पूर्णमुदच्यते ।
पूर्णस्य पूर्णमादाय पूर्णमेवावशिष्यते।।
ओं शांतिश्शांतिश्शांतिः ।।
श्रीगुरुभ्यो नमः ।
हरिःओम् । तत्सत् ।
श्रीकृष्णार्पणमस्तु ।।

oṁ pūrṇamadaḥ pūrṇamidaṁ pūrṇātpūrṇa-mudacyate ।
pūrṇasya pūrṇamādāya pūrṇamevāvaśiṣyate ।।
oṁ śāntiśśāntiśśāntiḥ ।।
śrīgurubhyo namaḥ ।
hariḥ oṁ । *tatsat* ।
śrīkṛṣṇārpaṇamastu ।।

Glossary

Ācārya : preceptor

Adharma : unrighteous action

Akhaṇḍacaitanya : the indivisible consciousness

Ahaṅkāra : ego sense

Anātman : non-self

Apohana : forgetting

Ātma Sākṣātkāra : realisation of the Self

Ātmadharma : the life committed to Self-knowledge

Ātmajñāna : Self-knowledge

Ātman : the Self

Ātmaniṣṭhā : abiding in the Self

Bahuvrīhi : the attributive compound

Bhakti : devotion

Bhoktṛtva : enjoyership

Buddhi : intellect

Brahmavidyā : knowledge of *Brahman*

Cetana, *Caitanya* : consciousness

Deha-abhimāna : identification with the body

Dharma : righteous action

Dhātu : basic ingredient

Indrīya : sense-organ

Īśvara : The Lord

Jaḍa : insentient

Jagat : universe

Jijñāsu : one who is desirous of knowing

Jīva : the individual

Jñānendriya : sense-organ

Kāraṇa : cause

Karma : activity

Karmadhāraya : descriptive compound

Karmendriya : organ of action

Kārya : effect

Karmī : one who is committed to performing rituals

Kartṛtva : doership

Kūrma : incarnation of the Lord in the form of a tortoise

Mahātmā : wise person

Manana : reflection

Matsya : incarnation of the Lord in the form of a fish

Māyā Śakti : the creative and delusive power of the Lord

Mokṣa : liberation

Nāma-rūpa : name and form

Navarasa : the nine sentiments in poetry or drama

Nirīśvaravādin : athiest scholar

Nididhyāsana : contemplation

Nirguṇa nirākāra : The Supreme Lord who is without

Parameśvara forms and attributes

Nirguṇa nirviśeṣa caitanya : attributeless formless aware-ness

Nirvikalpa : without divisions

Prārabdha : destiny

Prakṛti : material cause

Prāṇa : vital force

Pūjā : worship

Pūrṇa : complete

Rajas : activity, ambition

Rūpa : form

Sādhanā : means, practice

Sahasra nāma : thousand names

Saṁsāra : life of becoming

Saṁskāra : potential impression

Sādhaka : seeker

Śāstra : scripture

Sattva : harmony, peace

Savikalpa : with divisions

Śravaṇa : listening to the teaching from a Guru

Stotra : encomium

Sakala buddhi pratyaya sākṣī : witness to all thought modifications

Sthūladṛṣṭi : gross vision

Svarūpa : one's essential nature

Tamas : ignorance, laziness

Tatpadārtha : meaning of the word 'That'

Tvampadārtha : the meaning of the word thou

Upāsanā : meditation

Upāsaka : one who is committed to the meditation on the Lord with attributes

Vastu : Reality

Vikṣepa : agitation of the mind

Vyāmoha : delusion

Viśvarūpa upāsanā : contemplating on the comsic form of the Lord

Index